THE
PERFORMANCE
MANAGEMENT
HANDBOOK

Mike Walters is a principal consultant at ER Consultants. Prior to joining ER Consultants he worked in human resource management for Shell and for the BBC, and was a development manager with the then Institute of Personnel Management (now the Institute of Personnel and Development). His work as a consultant covers such areas as performance management, culture change, personnel policies and processes, and employee opinion surveys. His publications, as author or co-author, include *Changing Culture* (1993); *The Culture Factor* (1994); and *Employee Attitude and Opinion Surveys* (1996), all published by the IPD.

developing practice

Other titles in the series:

Counselling in the Workplace
Jenny Summerfield and Lyn van Oudtshoorn

Employee Attitude and Opinion Surveys
Mike Walters

The Job Evaluation Handbook
Michael Armstrong and Angela Baron

Project Management
Roland and Frances Bee

Re-engineering's Missing Ingredient
Mike Oram and Richard S Wellins

The Institute of Personnel and Development is the leading publisher of books and reports for personnel and training professionals and students and for all those concerned with the effective management and development of people at work. For full details of all our titles please telephone the Publishing Department on 0181 263 3387.

THE PERFORMANCE MANAGEMENT HANDBOOK

**Edited by
Mike Walters**

INSTITUTE OF PERSONNEL AND DEVELOPMENT

Design by Paperweight
Typeset by Action Typesetting Ltd, Gloucester
Printed in Great Britain by
The Cromwell Press, Wiltshire

British Library Cataloguing in Publication Data
A catalogue record for this book is available from the British
Library

ISBN 0-85292-579-4

**INSTITUTE OF PERSONNEL
AND DEVELOPMENT**

IPD House, Camp Road, London SW19 4UX
Tel: 0181 971 9000   Fax: 0181 263 3333
Registered office as above. Registered Charity No. 1038333
A company limited by guarantee. Registered in England No. 2931892

CONTENTS

ACKNOWLEDGEMENTS

It is never easy to draw together the work of several authors, particularly when the individuals concerned are busy people juggling numerous priorities. I would like to express my thanks to all the contributors to the book, and particularly express my gratitude for their co-operation in the face of whatever revisions and changes I have made to their work. We would all like to thank our colleagues for their help and ideas in developing the contents of the book.

I would also like to thank Margaret James of ER Consultants' Resource Centre in Cambridge for her help in putting together the reading list and for providing background information and references.

Finally, personal thanks as always to Christine and James for putting up with the absent evenings and weekends while I was serving my time as editor

Mike Walters

CONTRIBUTORS

Shirley Dalziel
Shirley Dalziel is a consultant at ER Consultants working primarily in the area of teambuilding, learning and development, stress management, and organisational change. Prior to joining ER Consultants, she was a lecturer at Glasgow Caledonian University, and she has carried out extensive research in the areas of individual and organisational learning. She also has management experience in the retail sector. Shirley is a chartered occupational psychologist, an Associate Fellow of the British Psychological Society, and a graduate of the Institute of Personnel and Development.

Ann Gammie
Ann is a principal consultant at ER Consultants, with extensive consultancy experience working in management development, TQM initiatives, communiation and attitude surveys, and process re-engineering projects in Europe and the United States. Ann is a graduate in psychology and has held appointments in accountancy and audit, as well as in training and organisation development, both in the public sector and in a high-technology sales and marketing organisation. She has written articles on TQM, training, and managing change.

Mairin Gannon
Mairin is manager – training and development at Polygram. Until recently she was a senior consultant at ER Consultants, with wide experience in human resource management and in learning and development activities. Her consultancy experience includes work on teambuilding, change management, upward feedback, and personal development planning. Prior to joining ER Consultants she worked for BP, facilitating a process

of significant cultural change over a three-year period. She has also held a variety of personnel and human resource management posts. She has a Bachelor of Science degree in psychology.

Peter Lawson

Peter Lawson is a senior consultant at ER Consultants. He has wide experience in operational and human resource management, having held senior line and functional management in the paper converting and distribution industries. Earlier in his career he held a number of management services/industrial engineering positions in the manufacturing sector. His consultancy experience covers areas such as performance measurement and management, the design and implementation of pay schemes, and a range of training and development assignments. Peter is a member of the Institute of Personnel and Development and the Institute of Management Services. He has been awarded a Bachelor of Arts degree by the Open University having graduated in the Social Sciences.

Ashley Richardson

Ashley Richardson is a senior consultant at ER Consultants, with many years of human resources experience in both consultancy and line management. Prior to joining ER he ran his own small consultancy, advising clients in pay matters, re-organisation and outplacement, and training. Earlier in his career Ashley was director of personnel for a manufacturing company after spending some years with Inbucon and Price Waterhouse. He has worked in Europe, Africa, and the Far East.

INTRODUCTION

Mike Walters

A couple of years ago, a colleague and I were working in a public-sector organisation whose senior management had expressed a desire for more effective performance management. As we walked round the organisation on our first visit, we were struck by the enthusiasm and industry evident among the employees. We commented on this, and asked what performance problems the organisation faced. The chief executive responded: 'Yes, they're certainly energetic enough. They all work hard and put in long hours. The trouble is, they just do what they want. They pursue their own projects, ride their own hobby-horses. We need to make sure not just that they produce good-quality work, but that it's what the organisation wants.'

This is one definition of performance management. It is not simply about working hard or working quickly. It is not even only about meeting individual objectives. It is about directing and supporting employees to work as effectively and efficiently as possible *in line with the needs of the organisation*.

We achieve effective performance management through a variety of tools and interventions at different levels in the organisation. These may include, for example:

- strategic planning
- the definition of organisational goals, priorities and values
- the identification and application of appropriate performance goals and measures for the organisation, for key processes, for functions, and for individual employees
- appraisal
- personal development planning
- learning and development activities
- various forms of performance-related pay.

The precise mix of these different activities varies from organisation to organisation, and may even vary within a single organisation, depending on the corporate needs and objectives that have been identified. Nevertheless, if we are to manage performance effectively, we need to ensure that our various interventions are co-ordinated and that all are aligned with organisational requirements.

This sounds uncontroversial, and yet, in practice, few organisations actually work like that. In most cases the tools of performance management are applied in a piecemeal and haphazard manner. Business strategy is defined in one part of the organisation, and no effort is made to identify its performance implications. Functional and process goals and measures are defined by individual managers, based on a limited understanding of the organisation's broader requirements. Individual performance measures are more fragmented still. The appraisal scheme has been in place for years, and does not reflect our current organisational needs. And we have introduced an output-based incentive bonus scheme because productivity must be a good thing.

Each of these interventions may be perfectly sound and sensible in its own right, but together they comprise considerably less than the sum of their parts. At best, they fail to reinforce one another (and so fail to reinforce the organisation's performance). At worst, they may be actively contradictory. As a result, the organisation underperforms, and its employees become confused and demotivated.

This book aims to help managers through this maze by developing a co-ordinated model of performance management that reflects both corporate objectives and key organisational interdependencies. The book is constructed to reflect the process that must underpin strategic performance management.

☐ In Chapter 1, Peter Lawson provides an overview of performance management and sets out some of its history and background. He concludes by outlining a systematic model of performance measurement.

☐ In Chapter 2, Mike Walters outlines some of the issues to be addressed in defining organisational measures, based on an understanding of organisational goals and priorities. He also highlights some of the potential pitfalls of organisational target setting.

☐ In Chapter 3, Ann Gammie explains the growing importance of processes in organisations, and sets out some of the tools for defining measures of process performance.

☐ In Chapter 4, Ann Gammie explores the challenges of setting individual performance goals and measures. She explores concepts of individual accountability and responsibility, and indicates some of the tensions inherent in establishing individual measures.

☐ In Chapter 5, Peter Lawson explains some of the principles of effective appraisal, with a particular focus on the value of '360-degree' appraisal. He also indicates how appraisal can be applied as an effective tool for managing and developing individual performance.

☐ In Chapter 6, Mairin Gannon sets out a systematic approach to personal development planning to be used as the basis for improving individual performance.

☐ In Chapter 7, Shirley Dalziel explores how the results of the personal development planning process can be translated into practical learning and development activities. She identifies some of the challenges involved in effective learning, and sets out their implications for learning and development activities.

☐ In Chapter 8, Ashley Richardson examines the role of performance-related pay in reinforcing (or undermining) performance management objectives. He considers various forms of performance-related pay, and assesses their relevance to particular performance needs.

☐ Finally, in Chapter 9, Mike Walters pulls together the various threads of the book, highlighting some key themes and learning points. This chapter also provides an extended case study, based on a number of real-life examples, designed to illustrate some practical applications of the ideas and approaches presented in the book.

We hope that this sequence represents a coherent and structured approach to performance management. We have nevertheless consciously provided a range of perspectives on the subject, and we hope that each chapter will promote organisational debate as well as providing some solutions. There is no simple prescription for effective performance management. Every organisation is different, and every organisation has different performance needs. For all that, we hope that this book provides some tools and some guiding principles to enable managers to develop approaches that will meet their particular needs.

1

PERFORMANCE MANAGEMENT: AN OVERVIEW

Peter Lawson

Words have a history just as we have a history, and the language that we use reflects the influences and the interests of our time. In the sixteenth century, for example, our understanding of the words *performance* and *management* would have reflected the militaristic preoccupations of the time. *Performance* meant the carrying out of commands or duties, and *management* referred, quite specifically, to the training of horses in the exercises of the *manège*.

Today, these words are widely used in management literature and in our everyday conversations at work, but they are not necessarily clearly understood. They are used, often with little precision, to describe a range of activities connected with the world of work. Definitions vary from organisation to organisation, from individual to individual, and our own understanding changes over time, reflecting differences in the interests and objectives of the organisations and societies in which we work.

Against this background, this book is an attempt to define and describe some very precise applications of the term Performance Management as it is used (and abused) as a tool to help us operate more effectively at work. Our aim is to develop a comprehensive and practical model of performance management, and to explore the tools and techniques needed to apply this model effectively.

Defining performance management

Let us begin by suggesting a straightforward, if loose, definition of 'performance management' which most people today would accept and understand. In simple terms, performance is about doing things, and management is about getting things done. There is a strong sense of activity in the former and a certain passivity in the latter. People *perform* and do things, and *managers* get things done by others. In other words, 'performance management' is about the arrangements organisations use *to get the right things done successfully*.

Our modern understanding of the concept of organisational and work management has its origins in North America. The term *management* was used to denote both a function and the people who carried out that function. It was also used to describe a social position and a field of academic study. In all cases, the context was essentially that of commercial business. Today we use and understand the term much more widely. The task of management is seen to apply not only to an industrial or commercial enterprise but also to institutions such as a university or a hospital. Even the village school and the voluntary association happily speak of their management and management committees or teams.

Management is essentially concerned with the search for superior organisational or business performance. The profit motive – the engine of capitalism – demands that businesses constantly search for improvement, and we are increasingly seeking similar improvements in the efficiency and effectiveness of public-sector and not-profit-making organisations. Sometimes this search leads the business and management community to work for change and development within the external climate in which they operate – for example, changes in legislation or in fiscal policy. Alongside this, though, managers need constantly to be reviewing their organisation's *internal* structures, systems and activities, in order to work towards continuing improvements in performance.

Management has always been about getting the job done, and good managers have always been looking for ways to get the right things done well. This is the essence of performance management – *the organisation of work to achieve optimum results*. At one level, performance management can be defined, quite simply, as the totality of the day-to-day work of managers. However, even a brief consideration of this apparently straightforward proposition begins to reveal its complexity. For example, if individual managers seek to optimise performance within their own areas of accountability without reference to the organisation at large, there is no certainty that they will all have the same priorities or objectives.

Furthermore, because the skills and abilities of individual managers are likely to vary considerably, so the levels of performance achieved will also vary. In response to this problem, the history of management is littered with people's attempts to evolve managerial processes and systems which capture best practice and place it at the disposal of all managers, in order to help ensure that individual management goals and achievements are supportive of the organisation's overall goals and objectives.

Nevertheless, despite a somewhat frantic and continuing search, no single approach or technique has, to date, been able to secure for managers what they so ardently desire – consistently high levels of organisational and managerial performance. In this context, it may be instructive to reflect briefly on the history of performance management.

One writer[1] has characterised the attempts to find this holy grail of superior performance as either of two, largely unrelated, approaches – one concerned with work processes and the other concerned with people. These approaches are based on a subdivision of management thinking into the scientific and human schools of management. The outcome of this categorisation was a list of process-focused techniques and a list of people-focused techniques which in theory are quite separate and distinct, but which in practice overlap.

The process approach is based on the notion that superior performance is achieved by analysing the work done in order to achieve predetermined results. This involved designing the most efficient method or sequence of work activities. Such an approach is supported by the 'certainty' that people at work are

[1] Alan Fowler, 'Performance Management: The MBO of the 90s', *Personnel Management*, July, 1990.

The Process Approach	The Human Approach
Work study	Selection test techniques
Critical path analysis	Training needs analysis
Operational research	Training techniques
Organisation and methods	Joint consultation
Performance planning and review	Industrial democracy
Cost benefit analysis	Merit rating
Job evaluation	Quality circles
Statistical manpower planning	Human resource planning
Management by objectives	Performance-related pay

rational beings, and that they will slavishly follow the prescribed methods simply because it has been demonstrated that this way of working is the best.

The people approach is predicated by the belief that superior performance can only be achieved through people. So if the right people are in the right jobs in the right numbers with the right skills, and if they are effectively led and motivated, the inevitable outcome is high performance. In this model it is assumed that such people in such circumstances develop their own best approach to the work that has to be done.

Many attempts have been made to develop comprehensive programmes or tools to achieve performance improvement by focusing on people or process issues. Examples include:

☐ *Work study* – In its most common usage, work study first of all sought to improve the way each task was carried out so that the single best way could be defined. Very often the next step in this process was to measure the work content of the defined task and to express that work content as a standard time for the completion of the task. The standard time had two uses. It was used in production planning and control systems to progress and cost work through the manufacturing process. It was also used in incentive schemes designed to encourage individuals and groups workers to improve their output by linking time to increases in their earnings. In practice, however, the outcome from such schemes tended to be increased earnings without a corresponding increase in output.

☐ *Management by objectives* – Although management by objectives also recognised the possible motivational effect on people at work of knowing what they were required to do, it was based on a rational approach to organisations, their structures, their operations and objectives. In essence, it was a systematic approach to letting people know what was required of them and how well they were doing in meeting this requirement. Initially the approach was widely welcomed as a practical solution to the challenges of performance management. Within 10 years of its creation, however, it had largely fallen into disuse. Its highly structured, bureaucratic approach was alien to many organisations. Moreover, because the emphasis was directed at the individual manager, objectives set in different departments of the same organisation were often incompatible. Above all, middle managers often saw it as a centrally imposed task irrelevant to their day-to-day concerns. As a result it tended to become a once-a-year exercise, unable to reflect the week-to-week changes that were of most concern to managers.

☐ *Critical path analysis* – This was once seen as the answer to all the problems of managing large and complex projects. In practice the conduct of complex projects was often incompatible with the disciplines required of the technique, and short cuts, unforeseen problems and delays in keeping the plan up to date meant that the plan was not an adequate guide. The validity and acceptability of the technique was thus undermined.

☐ *Merit rating* – Merit rating sought to motivate people to higher standards of performance through financial recognition. There is little or no evidence that it ever achieved its goal, probably because of the tenuous connections between the criteria against which people were rated and actual performance in the job.

☐ *Quality circles* – These were intended to raise organisa-tional performance through the involvement of employees in the improvement of work process and product quality. But employee involvement initiatives such as this were often applied in the alien environment of traditional 'command and control' organisations. Furthermore, many companies failed to realise that the talents of their people could be fully harnessed to their goal of quality or perfor-mance improvement only if they changed their work processes to match the new situation. Too often innovative, perhaps unconventional, ideas became submerged in formal procedure and processes for making, for example, design or manufacturing method changes.

There are a number of lessons we can draw from this brief review of failed attempts to find the panacea to the problem of performance management:

☐ People-based approaches to performance management must be underpinned by a supporting process. Enthusiasm is not enough. A procedural framework is required if good ideas are to be implemented quickly and efficiently.

☐ Process-based approaches must take into account the changes in attitude and skill required to make them operate effectively. The issue of 'ownership' is also critical, and such initiatives must be developed and imple-mented so as to ensure that all managers are involved and committed.

☐ Both people- and process-based approaches do not succeed if they are incompatible with the organisation's culture and way of doing things. Informal and flexible organisations reject highly structured approaches just as surely as command and control organisations reject collaborative or team-based approaches. The cultural implications of any approach must be fully worked out and taken into account as part of the implementation process of any initiative.

☐ Lastly, it should be noted that all the approaches and initia-tives so far discussed were *introspective* – that is, their emphasis required managers to look inwards into the inter-nal workings of the organisation, rather than requiring them to link the organisation and its operations to the external context of the business environment and the requirements of their customers.

Towards a new model of performance management

It is clear, therefore, that the establishment of effective mechanisms for performance management poses major challenges. At the same time, the issue of performance management has never been more pertinent. One of the most important business developments in the twentieth century was the emergence from the 1970s of a globally integrated economic system. The impact that this development has had on the competitive position of a great deal of Western European and North American business has been considerable, involving the loss of leadership positions in both home and export markets. Foreign competitors have simultaneously made substantial advances in several key sectors.

This loss of leadership has caused many businesses to review their own practice and look closely at the way that foreign, especially Japanese, corporate success has been achieved. What has emerged from these examinations is not only an urgent need to improve the performance of our businesses, but also an equally urgent need to improve the way in which business performance is measured and managed. Furthermore, the strong link between business performance management and business performance measurement must become more widely understood.

What however do we mean by 'business performance'?

Too often the term is little more than a vacuous buzzword. One commentator has suggested that current interest in performance arises because the word 'exudes an aroma of action, dynamism and purposeful effort. It suggests the sorting out of the good from the bad.'[2]

In reality, the word *performance* has different meaning for

---

[2] C. Politt, 'Beyond the Managerial Model: The case for broadening assessment in government and the public services', *Financial Accountability and Management*, 1986.

different audiences. For some the focus may be on financial performance; for others the focus may be policy effectiveness. Some may be more interested in business process performance, whereas consumers are concerned with the quality of products or with the delivery of services.

However we define the term, the business community has shown considerable interest in identifying the source of superior organisational performance. This interest has spawned a massive literature of the *In Search of Excellence* genre which attempts to identify the ingredients of success from an analysis of performance over time. Many have alternatively looked towards Japan, believing that Japanese business success provided the key. In fact such authors found that the art of Japanese management was not exclusively Japanese at all, but embraced the humanistic management practices of many Western organisations

It is now becoming clear that each function, department or work centre must understand, manage and improve those aspects of its performance that best enable the company or organisation to achieve its aims, goals and objectives. Although there are several models of performance, one that is particularly useful depicts performance as a pyramid[3] in which is contained the objectives and measures that connect an organisation's corporate vision, values and objectives to its day-to-day operations (see Figure 1).

The right-hand half of the pyramid, which reflects the organisation's internal focus, is dominated, not surprisingly, by traditional financial and other productivity performance concerns and measures. These are valid and important both for the business as a whole and for its constituent parts. However, managers are increasingly recognising that these measures represent only a partial view of the performance picture. Alongside them, there is a need to include market-

---

[3] The 'performance pyramid' has been adapted from an article entitled 'For Good Measure', by Kelvin Cross, BA, MA, and Richard Lynch, MBA, BS (Finance), which appeared in *CMA* magazine, April 1992, and is reprinted with the permission of the Society of Management Accountants of Canada. It is also used by Cross and Lynch in their book *Measure Up ... How to measure corporate performance*, London, Blackwell, 2nd edition, 1995.

Figure 1
THE 'NEW' PERFORMANCE PARADIGM

- Internal focus
- External focus
- Integrated
- Global competition
- Diffused focus

focused concerns and measures, as well as an increased emphasis on the way in which traditional measures are converted into day-to-day operational activity.

Market share is of critical importance. Some recent Japanese successes may be attributed to their greater emphasis on the market. The Japanese tend to measure performance in terms of current market share and the ratio of new products (future market share) rather than simply relying on return on investment as a monolithic measure of performance. Many British and American managers focus on financial measures first, market share second, and future market share – if at all – as a very distant third.

At the top of the pyramid is the company's vision (goals) and values. These express its spirit, life and soul. An organisation's vision is nothing less than a statement of the way it wishes to do business – for example, defining its markets and how it intends to compete, whether on price, on breadth of product range, or on the range and quality of its services.

The second level of the pyramid – the level of the business unit – comprises the organisation's key result areas, objectives and measures. Most business units define success in two ways: first, by reaching short-term targets of cash flow and profitability, and secondly, achieving longer-term goals of growth and market position. Market measures, defined by customers, might include absolute or relative market share compared to the position of major competitors.

The business processes at the heart of the model provide a bridge between the top-level traditional performance indicators and the new day-to-day operational measures. This stratum includes all the internal functions, activities, policies, procedures and supporting systems needed to develop, produce and provide specific goods and services for specific customer needs. For example, distinct business operating processes exist for product definition and development, for sales order processing, for customer service, and for credit control.

In this way, business processes link *department* performance with *company* strategy and performance, by measuring not just the efficiency of single departments but the effectiveness of *all* the business processes involved.

One department may be involved in several business processes – for example, a customer service department may be involved in the sales order process as well as estimating and credit control processes. Each business process may have very different objectives and indicators of successful performance. Understanding the operation of each process, however, enables the development of effective departmental performance measures and facilitates links between departmental and organisational performance.

The main business process performance indicators are likely to be customer satisfaction, flexibility, and productivity.

☐ *Customer satisfaction* – The difference between expectation and performance, this indicates how well both customer expectations and product/service delivery are managed.

☐ *Flexibility* – This lies at the heart of the performance pyramid, for it defines how responsive business processes are to changing customer requirements. Many Japanese companies assign the highest priority to flexibility.

□ *Productivity* – This denotes how effectively resources, including time, are managed to achieve customer satisfaction and flexibility objectives.

At the base of the pyramid are the specific measures of performance which managers and employees can monitor and control on a daily basis.

As the model suggests, each level of performance is linked to those above and below. High-quality products or services and regular on-time delivery lead to customer satisfaction. The combination of externally driven delivery (when the customer wants to take delivery) and internally driven cycle times (optimising machine change and machine run times) defines flexibility. Productivity can be enhanced by reducing cycle times and waste. At the departmental level, waste includes those resources and activities that add no value but are incurred while meeting other performance objectives.

Efforts to improve performance often emphasise one dimension of performance at the expense of another – for example, quality at any price, or improving on-time delivery by allowing the inventory to rise. Managers now recognise a requirement to develop and manage an integrated 'basket' of performance measures simultaneously. The objective of any department or function must be to manage business processes which enhance quality and delivery while reducing cycle time and waste. There is an obvious need to understand how these performance criteria behave and interact – a theme we return to frequently in this book.

Performance measures are either internal, and therefore invisible to customers (cycle time and waste), or external, and visible and important to customers (quality and delivery).

The four core performance measures are often managed simultaneously, sometimes by concentrating attention on one measure while merely monitoring others. The actual focus of attention depends on a number of factors – for instance, the difference between the company's performance and the performance of the company's competition, or the relative rate of the company's improvement in performance relative to that of the company's competitors. It is not enough to set arbitrary static performance targets such as '95 per cent stock availability'. Such a goal is positively dangerous if it is regularly exceeded by the competitors.

In competitive markets, meaningful improvement arises from managing key performance indicators. An organisation must compare its rate of improvement with that of its most combative rivals *in the dimensions of performance which define its competitive position*. Furthermore, it is often not good enough simply to outperform the competitors; what is required is the ability to compete with best practice in *any* organisation. Some organisations demand that all their departments and functions 'benchmark' their performance against leaders in the field regardless of industry or sector.

Whatever your performance indicators tell you, it is very risky to allow your attention to be diverted from particular performance measures just because you believe performance is satisfactory at present. Complacency can lead to competitive disasters. Comparable competitor performance may surge while your attention is diverted so that even continuous performance improvement may be too late to save the day. What may be required in this situation is a 'breakthrough' performance improvement in which aggressive and ambitious goals – a 50 per cent reduction in the time to bring a new product to market, say, or a 90 per cent reduction in machine change time – are introduced.

Examples of 'breakthrough' performance are:

☐ the circuit-board assembly plant which reduced in-process cycle time from 30 to 3 days and improved first-pass yield to 85 per cent from 65 per cent within a few weeks

☐ a 50 per cent reduction in the backlog of invoices by establishing semi-autonomous work teams responsible for the entire billing process.

In summary, effective performance management means.

☐ articulating your company's vision

☐ establishing key results, objectives and measures at business unit level

☐ identifying business process objectives and the key indicators of performance for those processes

□ identifying and installing effective departmental measures

□ monitoring and controlling four key performance measures

□ managing the continuous improvement of performance in those key areas – 'benchmarking' your performance against the best

□ being prepared to aim for 'breakthrough' improvements in performance when this is required by a significant shortfall in your performance measured against the performance of your major competitors.

The performance pyramid model demonstrates how the top-level corporate vision is driven down, through and across business units via an interlinked network of performance measures that reflect both internal and external effectiveness. Performance management thus addresses not only internally focused financial and productivity performance, but also externally focused performance in such areas as market share, customer satisfaction, flexibility, quality, and the delivery of products and services.

Integrated and coherent business performance measurement and management processes are a powerful tool in delivering successful business strategies. If they are dedicated to meeting customer requirements, supporting strategic business objectives, and integrated at all levels of the organisation, performance measures allow managers to identify and manage those day-to-day priorities that ensure superior performance.

This model and vision of performance management and measurement suggests that the task of managers is concerned with *connectivity*. It is about identifying, building upon, and strengthening the connections that link the organisation, its managers and its employees with its customers and markets. These connections include business processes, relevant scientific and technical knowledge, and, most importantly, the network of human relationships between managers, colleagues, suppliers, customers and shareholders.

Building, modifying as required, and rebuilding all these connections over time in response to a rapidly changing world is the management task of the twenty-first century, and upon our success in this endeavour our society critically depends. We shall address in detail some key components of this task.

2

DEVELOPING ORGANISATIONAL MEASURES

Mike Walters

The way we work and the way we manage are increasingly subject to measurement. In a growing number of organisations, across all parts of the economy, employees are required to carry out their day-to-day activities against a framework of formal goals and measures. The terminology varies from organisation to organisation – strategic measures, critical success factors, performance indicators, key indices, 'the dials in the cockpit', 'the critical few' – but the intention is generally similar. The aim is to underpin all our work activities with systematic measures that enable the organisation to assess whether we are performing effectively and how our performance can be improved.

In many respects, this trend towards measurement is welcome. Traditionally, many organisations – private and public sector alike – have not been good at gathering performance data. Whether as managers or consultants, we have all encountered the frustration arising from poor (or non-existent) performance measurement. How much does this activity cost? How is that investment justified? How efficient is this process? What are the main bottlenecks in that operation? All too often, the answer has been that no one knows, that the information is not available, or that it would take too long to find out. Where information has existed, it has tended to be largely financial. We might know to the last penny how much was invested in new plant, new working methods, or in developing the employees, but we have had little inkling of how much (if at all) this improved performance.

In moving towards more systematic measurement, therefore, managers are recognising the truth behind the old cliché that 'If you aren't measuring it, you aren't managing it.' We have begun to recognise that effective management depends upon a precise understanding of our performance, in all its aspects and in all parts of the organisation and its processes. In many organisations, as we see elsewhere in this book, managers are now striving to evaluate performance at many levels, including:

☐ contribution to the achievement of strategic objectives

☐ measures of quality

☐ measures of quantity and volume

☐ measures of efficiency and value for money

☐ measures of external and internal customer satisfaction.

By applying these and other measures, managers are aiming to build up a multidimensional picture of their organisations' performance in order to build on those areas in which the organisation is performing well and to identify those areas in which there is scope for improvement.

Expressed in these terms, the benefits of effective performance measurement appear self-evident. And yet, in practice, the impact of performance measurement has often been much less positive. In many parts of the public sector, for example, the introduction of formal performance measurement has been treated with a high level of suspicion and cynicism. There has, for example, been widespread resistance to the development of the 'charter' concept, with its emphasis on measurable standards of customer service. Equally, in such areas as health and education, the application of performance 'league tables' has been greeted with, at best, scepticism and, at worst, resentment and anger. And in both the public and the private sectors alike, some aspects of performance measurement – its link with individual appraisal, its potential links with pay – remain highly controversial. We discuss many of these issues elsewhere in this book.

The challenges of performance measurement

The reasons for this resistance to performance measurement are various. In many organisations there is concern about the 'hidden agenda' that may underlie the introduction of more systematic forms of performance measurement. Performance measurement is perceived as a prelude to a range of more threatening developments – privatisation, perhaps, or cost-cutting, or staffing reductions. Often, of course, such concern is justified. The desire to improve performance measures may well be part of a much wider drive towards improved organisational performance in a number of areas.

Moreover, regardless of the context, performance measurement is a threatening concept in its own right. We may be confident that we are doing a good job, but we may still not want to have our confidence put to the test. This sense of threat is likely to be most acute in those areas – such as internal service functions – that have traditionally not been subject to systematic measurement. In the past there may have been little formal definition even of individual role or purpose, let alone of individual performance measures. As measures are introduced, employees may feel that the very basis of their contribution to the organisation is being questioned.

At heart, though, this widespread anxiety about the impact and implications of performance measurement perhaps reflects a more fundamental issue. Quite simply, *it is extremely difficult to measure performance effectively*. Despite the superficial allure of performance measurement – 'If we measure things better, we'll be able to manage them better' – in practice the process often proves highly problematic. Many organisations have developed sophisticated strategic planning frameworks, but rather fewer have succeeded in translating them into convincing measures of performance across the organisation.

There are reasons for this. First, work performance is rarely monolithic. In most cases, effective performance comprises a portfolio of disparate achievements – meeting deadlines, juggling priorities, delivering quality, and so on. If we attempt to measure all aspects of the job, we may well end up with an unwieldy (and perhaps even potentially contradictory) basket of different measures. Conversely, if we select only those aspects we perceive as most important, we risk undervaluing some potentially critical areas of performance.

Even for jobs with a relatively precise performance focus, this equation is often far from straightforward. Most organisations have, for example, long applied formal performance measurement to their sales staff. After all, the only purpose of a salesperson is to sell, so it is reasonable to evaluate performance on the basis of how much he or she sells. The difficulties inherent in this simple assertion can be illustrated by the respective examples of two companies facing contradictory problems in measuring sales performance.

In the first, sales performance was measured primarily on the basis of volume sold, and sales staff were given considerable latitude to adjust prices to achieve sales. Not surprisingly, the company soon found that although the sales people continued to earn their performance-related bonuses, its overall margins were increasingly being squeezed. In the second company, by contrast, because the company was operating at the premium end of its particular market, sales performance was evaluated substantially on the basis of maintaining margins. Predictably enough, the company found that its sales volume was increasingly being squeezed at the expense of sustaining its margins.

These are, of course, very simple – though real – examples, and both companies have now developed more sophisticated means of measuring sales performance. Nevertheless, they illustrate that even in a relatively straightforward field the identification of appropriate performance measures is likely to be a matter of balance and compromise. In defining performance measures for sales staff we need to balance a range of factors – volumes against margins, immediate sales against long-term repeat business, and so on. The precise balance will probably shift as the organisation's requirements and objectives change.

Even if we manage to identify an appropriate basket of performance measures for a specific role, it may still be difficult to develop consistent and effective measures for the workforce as a whole. We might, for example, wish to seek different types of performance from respective members of a given workteam, particularly if we are trying to encourage complementary contributions to team objectives. We may, for example, be looking for one team member to provide creative ideas, another to develop these into practical proposals, a third to manage the delivery of these proposals, and so on. How, then, do we go about measuring the performance of team members? Do we apply different standards and measures to different individuals, and so risk a charge of inconsistency or unfairness? Do we simply focus on the team's performance as a whole, and if so, how do we manage variations in individual contributions? Ann Gammie discusses a number of these issues in more detail in Chapter 4.

Even more important, we need to recognise both the diversity and the linkage between the various work-groups, departments and functions operating in the organisation. In each case we need to identify performance measures that reflect the distinct role and purpose of each group. At the same time, we also need to ensure that all the measures are mutually reinforcing and that all, ultimately, support the achievement of our strategic objectives. This may sound obvious, but there are countless organisations where the *totality* of individual performance measures serves to undermine, rather than enhance, corporate performance. We have all seen examples of organisations in which production staff are measured primarily on the basis of output (regardless of quality), sales staff are measured primarily on the basis of orders taken (regardless of whether the order can be met), managers are measured primarily on the basis of reducing costs (regardless of the long-term impact on perfor- mance) – and at the end of it all the organisation proclaims itself a 'total quality company'! Part of the solution to these problems, as Ann Gammie suggests in Chapters 3 and 4, is to adopt a process focus in the organisation, enabling us to focus our performance goals and measures on meeting our customers' needs. Even this, however, does not fully deal with the issue of how we integrate between processes, or how we integrate between current process delivery and future process development.

Pragmatists may argue that these problems do not matter. After all, performance management is not an exact science, and it is surely better to apply some measures, however imper- fect, rather than none at all. Up to a point this is probably true. No organisation develops effective performance measures immediately, and there will almost certainly be a need for amendment and refinement on the basis of practical experience.

It is worth stressing, nevertheless, that poor performance measurement is likely to be worse than none at all. While it is true that 'If you can't measure it, you can't manage it', it is also true, conversely, that 'What gets measured, gets managed'. And what gets managed, ultimately, dictates how people behave. In other words, if you are measuring the wrong things, you will encourage people to *do* the wrong things, especially if the measurement also influences their pay. This in turn may drag the organisation further and further from its corporate objectives. By the time you realise that the performance measures are inappropriate, you may well find that the organisation has developed a wealth of dysfunctional systems, structures and practices which cannot easily be dismantled.

In other words, regardless of how you ultimately use the resulting performance information, performance measurement is unlikely to be a neutral process. If you set measures that are inappropriate to organisational needs or objectives, you will encourage inappropriate behaviour. If you set unclear or confused measures, you will simply demotivate employees. If you set inconsistent measures in different parts of the organisation, you will undermine organisational effectiveness. Let us consider, then, how to meet these challenges and to set measures that will enhance individual and organisational performance.

Establishing the organisational context

The first rule is that all performance measures – whether for individuals, teams, departments or functions – need to reflect the wider organisational context. Measures cannot be set in isolation, but must take account both of wider organisational objectives and of interactions with other parts of the organisation.

Although simply stated, it may be not easy to achieve in practice. In recent years there has been a tendency for comprehensive and systematic approaches to performance management – such as management by objectives, discussed by Peter Lawson in Chapter 1 – to become discredited because they are perceived as overly centralised and bureaucratic. As many organisations move increasingly towards concepts of devolution, empowerment and federalisation, greater systematisation is unlikely to be welcome.

In establishing the context for developing performance measures, however, the emphasis should not be on complexity or bureaucracy but rather on *thoroughness and clarity*. In other words, there is no need for highly detailed statements of performance requirements at any level in the organisation, but there does need to be a precise statement of the organisation's overall needs. This in turn needs to be based on a full consideration, by the senior team, of the organisation's role, purpose and objectives.

The key questions here are likely to include:

☐ What are our organisational objectives? What do we wish to achieve, and over what time-scale?

☐ How do we prioritise these objectives? Do we expect this prioritisation to change over time?

☐ What kinds of qualities are needed to deliver these objectives? What are the implications in terms of corporate skills and competencies, values, behaviours and working styles?

☐ What are our current strengths and weaknesses in relation to these objectives? What do we need to change or develop in order to achieve our goals?

☐ What specific contributions do we require from particular parts of the organisation?

In many organisations these issues will have been addressed already as part of the strategic planning process, and may well be enshrined in business plans and in statements of mission, goals and values. But even if much of the groundwork has already been carried out these questions may well be worth revisiting from the perspective of performance measurement. The aim should be to move away from broad statements about business performance towards precise statements about what the organisation needs to do to deliver that business performance. In other words, what are the organisation's specific performance and development objectives, and what qualities are needed to deliver those objectives?

The emphasis should also be on prioritisation. In an ideal world we would all like everything – minimum costs, maximum production, premium quality, growing market share, the development of new markets, and so on. In practice, our resources and capability are always limited, and we need to focus on those areas that are likely to bring most benefit to the organisation. This does not necessarily mean, however, that we should focus on one issue at the expense of everything else. It may be important for us to improve quality, but it may be equally important to ensure that costs do not go out of control in the process. In short, we need to identify our priorities but we also need to be realistic about the broader picture and its associated constraints.

Examples of priorities identified might include:

☐ 'In the face of erosion in our current markets, our priority is to move into new market areas, which in turn requires the development of new products. We therefore need the highest capability in the various aspects of new product development...'

☐ 'Our priority is to reduce costs in order to ensure competitiveness. We therefore need to ensure that at all times we are making the most efficient use of both our plant and our employees...'

☐ 'Our priority is to improve customer perceptions of the quality of our products. This means both that we have to improve the actual quality of our products, and also to improve our relationship with our customers so that we have a better understanding of their needs and expectations...'

The scope and nature of the priorities identified of course vary dramatically from organisation to organisation. In general, though, it is probably unrealistic for most organisations to work towards more than three or four major objectives, of which only one or two involve significant development. The organisation might, for example, set a challenging target in terms of new product development, and some relatively low-level improvement targets in, say, quality improvement or cost reduction. Whereas it may be tempting to set demanding targets across all the organisation's activities, in practice this is likely to become simply a wish list which, as a basis for measuring performance, will only confuse and demotivate employees.

This last point should always be the acid test. What are the implications of this particular objective for employee performance? If we are to achieve that particular organisational goal, what kind and level of performance will we need? The implications of the answer then need to be considered in depth. If, for example, the organisation's focus is to be on new product development, then this carries a wide range of implications, all of which have potential ramifications in terms of individual performance. There may be a need to assess whether the organisation's culture and structure is suited to encouraging innovation. There may be a need to consider whether the organisation has the appropriate range and level of skills, both in technical areas and in the management of innovation. There may be a need to look at the organisation's capability in translating innovation into practical products, and in bringing these products effectively to the market-place. There may be a need to address the organisation's competence in identifying market needs or in collecting and analysing customer feedback.

By reviewing these various ramifications in detail, the organisation should be able to identify its performance priorities. These may well vary over time, so that, for example, the short-term priorities may be different from (although complementary to) the longer-term requirements. Over the next 12 months the priority might be to develop an organisational structure that enables innovation to take place, perhaps by separating innovative activity from day-to-day operations. During this period, therefore, the priorities for performance might focus on areas such as the management of change, the identification of individuals with innovation skills, the establishment and leadership of new work-groups, and so on. In the longer term, following the formation of the new structure, performance priorities might diverge between those staff involved in day-to-day operations and those involved in innovation, very different types of performance being required in different parts of the organisation.

In working through these issues, in order to ensure that the process maintains a practical focus, it may be helpful to think in terms of desired *outcomes*. In other words, what practical result does the organisation wish to see emerging at the end of the specified time-scale? It is then possible to work back towards the intermediary outcomes required to deliver the end result. This does not need to be a highly detailed process but does need to set some broad quantitative and qualitative targets. In this case, for example, the sequence might be:

By end of 12 months	To establish the organisation structure needed to promote new product development, including market research processes, innovation unit, robust processes for feasibility/market testing, and efficient processes for bringing products to market
By end of 24 months	To have developed a minimum of 30 product ideas which meet specified quality criteria
By end of 36 months	To have brought 10 products successfully to market, meeting defined product performance criteria

In practice, the establishment of these targets is likely to result from successive amendments as the feasibility of each objective is tested. In this case, for example, the key development steps and attendant questions might include:

☐ the establishment of a systematic development and implementation plan for creating the new organisation (*Will it really be feasible to establish the new structure in 12 months? What resources will be required? What will be the major barriers?*)

☐ the establishment of quality criteria to assess new product ideas (*Will it really be feasible to develop 30 ideas which meet these criteria?*)

☐ the establishment of criteria to assess market performance of new products (*Will 30 ideas be sufficient to generate 10 products which meet the defined performance criteria? Will it really be feasible to develop 10 successful products?*).

In developing these plans it is also crucial that we identify significant constraints. For example, what resources are available for research and development? What kinds of standards do we need to maintain in producing and selling our *existing* products, alongside the development of our new ideas? If we are to maintain or improve our performance across all our existing activities, do we need to compromise our more demanding development targets?

Once full consideration has been given to these issues for each of the priority objectives, the final stage is to consider the implications of the plans across the range of the organisation's activities. Depending on the nature of the priorities and the structure of the organisation, it might be appropriate to review these implications by function or discipline, by process, or across different parts of the business. In the case of new product development, for instance, we should review the different performance implications for, say, research and development, marketing, sales, operations, and so on. These are likely to vary significantly between different areas and also, possibly, over time. In the short term, for example, we may be looking for marketing and sales to maximise revenue from our existing products in order to support our research and development activity. In the longer term we may be looking to these functions to develop imaginative marketing and sales plans for the new products that are emerging. Again, the aim at this stage should not be to develop detailed plans for delivering these goals but simply to identify broad qualitative and quantitative targets and their performance implications.

We might map these performance targets systematically:

Function	Time-scales		
	12 months	24 months	36 months +
R&D			
Marketing			
Sales			
Production			
Finance			
HR			

By mapping the performance targets systematically in this way, we not only provide a basis for developing more detailed performance measurements within each area, we can also identify any potential inconsistencies or contradictions across the organisation as a whole. We need to ask, for example, how closely the performance measurements that emerge from this planning process match those that are in place currently. For example, it may be that performance in operations is currently measured on the basis of output of standard products. If the organisation is moving towards producing new, more customised products, then these measures may need to be revised. Similar steps may also be necessary in sales and marketing if the organisation is aiming to enter new markets and introduce customers to unfamiliar products.

All too often organisations attempt to introduce new objectives in some parts of their operations but retain traditional goals and measures in others. Our research and marketing staff are busy developing new products, but our sales and production staff are still measured on how efficiently they deliver the old. As a result, they are reluctant to risk achieving their performance targets by focusing on our new requirements.

By mapping these performance relationships systematically we can try to ensure that we are applying performance measures that are consistent across the organisation and that develop in line with our organisational needs. Such mapping may also indicate a need for some more radical changes to the organisation in order to ensure that consistency is achieved. If there are significant performance dependencies between different functions or disciplines, for instance, it may be appropriate to restructure the organisation so that these are more effectively co-ordinated. This kind of thinking underlies the increasing development of process-based organisation, as Ann Gammie discusses in more detail in Chapter 3.

Conversely, if we feel that there is a significant disparity between performance objectives in different parts of the organisation, we may feel that it is appropriate to separate these structurally – for example, separating the delivery of our traditional business from the development of new products and services. These implications lie beyond the scope of this book, but the key message remains the same. We should have a full understanding of the organisational context within which individual performance measurement takes place, so that we know and can clearly communicate what we require of employees at all levels and in all parts of the organisation.

Relating organisational measures to the individual

We have consciously devoted considerable attention to the organisational context within which performance management takes place. Problems with the measurement and management of performance most frequently arise not because of problems with the handling of individual performance measures (although there may be problems here too), but because too little effort has been made to understand organisational priorities and dilemmas. All too often we hear employees complain, 'I don't know what the organisation wants of me. It says that we should improve quality, but then it won't let me fill half the jobs in my department because of cost constraints,' or, 'They tell me they want me to sell all these new, unfamiliar products, but they're ready to rap me on the knuckles if I don't exceed last year's sales targets.' These are not complaints about unsatisfactory performance targets set by the local manager. They are complaints about a lack of clarity about organisational needs and objectives. If our needs are not clear at the organisation level, we cannot hope to set effective performance measures for individual employees.

For all that, even when the organisation has succeeded in clarifying its corporate objectives we still face some difficulties in translating these into measures that can be devolved down the organisation. In order to develop effective measures of individual performance we need to balance a number of different, and potentially even contradictory, requirements.

First, we need to ensure that the measures we set appropriately reflect the organisation's overall priorities. The implications of this of course depend on the nature of these priorities and the diversity of employee contributions to the organisation as a whole. In most organisations, it is probably impossible to identify a single, one-dimensional measure that appropriately reflects the organisation's performance needs. Although, for ease of administration, we may be tempted to adopt the simplest measure, the likelihood is that it will be a simplistic distortion of our real performance needs. If we measure sales performance purely in terms of sales volumes, we may for instance discourage sales staff from selling the new products which are the real key to our future development. If we measure production purely in terms of output volumes, we may demotivate production staff faced with the challenges of producing unfamiliar products which, in the short term, reduce productivity.

If we do decide to focus on a single measure of performance, we need to ensure that we fully understand the implications. We may, for example, feel that this particular aspect of performance is such an important priority that we are prepared to live with a negative impact in other areas. If we need to make dramatic improvements in productivity, we may feel that it is worth sacrificing performance in such areas as quality or product development. Alternatively, we may believe that effective managers should be able to manage performance in those areas where there are no formal measurements in place. This may be true, but experience suggests that when the chips are down even the best managers sacrifice performance in unmeasured areas in order to deliver the figures.

In most cases, therefore, we will wish to apply a basket of measures, selected and weighted to reflect organisational priorities. Effective performance is measured not merely by the delivery of results (however outstanding) in one area but by delivering satisfactory performance across all the measures. Sales staff may have significantly exceeded their sales volume targets, but their performance is not satisfactory if their average margins have slipped below the acceptable level. Production staff may have dramatically exceeded their productivity targets, but their performance is not acceptable if the number of rejects or the level of customer complaints has dropped below the tolerance level.

These baskets of measures may be constructed to varying levels of sophistication. At the simplest level we may merely define acceptable performance standards across the relevant areas. We may also define higher-level targets, which may be used to gradate various forms of performance-related pay. We may allow employees some freedom to mix-and-match between the various measures within certain pre-defined limits. It might for example be acceptable for sales staff to sacrifice some margin in order to achieve higher sales volumes, or vice versa. Some organisations combine several measures, appropriately weighted in line with organisational priorities, to define a single index which is then used as the key measure of performance. This can work well, so long as it is carefully calculated and its implications are fully understood by the employees involved.

This brings us to the second essential characteristic of effective performance management. We need to ensure that the measures, and their implications, are clearly understood by the employees to whom they are applied. This means that

- ☐ employees should be made fully aware of all the measures that are being applied to them
- ☐ employees should understand the relative significance and weighting of the various measures
- ☐ employees should be aware of any specific performance targets or benchmark levels that have been set
- ☐ employees should be informed of their performance against the measures on a continuing basis.

The last point is particularly important. Employees should not suddenly discover at the end of the year that they have failed to achieve the defined performance target. Continuing performance data should be made available, and potentially unsatisfactory performance should be addressed at the earliest opportunity.

Above all, although we need to ensure that the chosen measures appropriately reflect organisation priorities, we must also ensure that the overall range of measures does not become overcomplicated. Most of us are unable to respond sensibly to more than three or four priority measures. Set more than this, we are likely either to become confused and demotivated or simply to make our own judgements about which ones are the most important. In doing so we may decide to disregard those that are actually most important to the organisation!

The key message therefore is 'Keep it simple'. For this reason, performance measurement almost always involves a compromise. We may well identify a dozen aspects of performance which, in an ideal world, we would like to manage and improve. In practice we have to make hard choices about our real priorities, even if this means devoting less attention to some aspects of performance. In making such decisions, however, we need to ensure that our chosen measures really do reflect organisational needs, and that we have not simply chosen those that are, say, easiest to collect or least threatening to apply.

This last point is critical. It is not unusual for organisations to apply a particular measure simply because the data is already available ('We know how many customer complaints we get, so let's use that as a measure of quality.') or simply because they feel comfortable with particular measures ('Well, I know *I* always hit my targets in that particular area, so it seems a reasonable one to apply to everyone else.'). In practice these measures may be telling them very little about the performance issues that are really important to the organisation.

At times, the identification of the most appropriate performance measures may require some careful thought and even ingenuity. You may need to define your terms with some precision. If, for example, you wish to identify appropriate measures of 'quality', the first question to ask is 'How do we define quality in this organisation?' Is it conformity with specification or with customer requirements? Is it a minimum of customer complaints? Is it a minimum of rejects at the quality-control stage? It may be any or all of these, but until we have defined our terms we cannot know which is the most appropriate measure for our needs.

Applying performance measures

If we are unable to measure performance effectively, we are unlikely to be able to manage it effectively. At the same time, we need to exercise some care in the way we use performance measures. Above all, it is important to stress that performance measurement, however and wherever it is carried out, should never be applied simply as a punitive tool. It should be a tool to improve understanding, to help identify where and why performance problems are occurring, and how best to respond to them.

It is easy to assume that if an employee repeatedly fails to achieve his or her performance targets the employee is at fault. It may be true – but we should look at the full facts before we jump to conclusions. We need to look, first of all, at the overall pattern of performance in the organisation. If a substantial number are underperforming, perhaps the problem is systemic rather than individual. Perhaps there are organisational problems to be resolved; perhaps we are simply recruiting the wrong people into the job; or perhaps our defined standards are unrealistic (in which case, we have to consider what alternatives are available to us).

We must also consider the extent to which employees are able fully to influence the measures we have set. Perhaps the employees' achievement of the performance measures has been influenced by factors outside their control – for example, problems at other points in the supply chain, or problems with the particular area or market in which the individual is operating. Perhaps employees are hindered by unsatisfactory equipment, or are not being appropriately supported by senior management. In the first instance, the aim should be to use the performance measures as a tool to help explore these issues – with employees, with their manager, and across the organisation as a whole.

If employees feel that their performance is being judged on the basis of measures that are not fully within their control, they can only end up feeling demotivated. If, on the other hand, they feel that the measures are being used to help overcome barriers to effective organisational performance, the credibility of the measurement process is enhanced.

This does not mean that individuals should not be held accountable for delivering results, or that we should ignore unsatisfactory individual performance. Indeed, as Ann Gammie indicates in Chapter 4, accountability and responsibility are always critical concepts in individual performance management. But it does mean that we should not assume that performance management is simply about managing the performance of individuals. Instead, we should recognise that, in general, performance problems are just as likely (if not more likely) to be caused by weaknesses in organisational systems and processes than by individual failings.

Finally, we need continually to review the performance measures themselves. As we have stressed throughout this chapter, performance measurement is rarely an exact science but is often a matter of subjective judgement and imperfect compromises. We should not therefore be seduced by the use of 'metrics', 'ratios' and 'indices' into assuming that the process is based on some inviolable scientific principles. We need constantly to be asking:

☐ Are we measuring the right things?
☐ Do our measures still reflect organisational priorities?
☐ Are we measuring what we think we are measuring?
☐ Do employees understand and accept the measures we are applying?
☐ Are our targets realistic (or, indeed, are they too low)?

Above all, we need to refer back to the organisational context. If we are performing satisfactorily against our defined performance measures, is this reflected in overall organisational performance? If it is not, either we have failed to identify the appropriate measures in the first place, or organisational needs and priorities have subsequently changed. Whichever, we need to rethink the way we measure performance.

Performance measurement is, quite simply, a tool to help us manage and improve organisational effectiveness. If it is applied thoughtfully and systematically, it can be a powerful mechanism for helping to identify and overcome barriers to effective performance. If it is applied carelessly (as it so often is), its effects may be not merely unhelpful but actually damaging because it drags the organisation into a cycle of inappropriate behaviour. As so often in management, the secret lies in the preparation – in making sure that we really understand our organisational needs. If we get that first step right, the rest will follow.

3

DEVELOPING PROCESS MEASURES

Ann Gammie

We must first examine what a process is and how it can be measured. The following diagram captures the essence of a process, and provides a basic definition:

Figure 2

A PROCESS TAKES INPUTS AND TRANSFORMS THEM INTO OUTPUTS, ADDING VALUE ON THE WAY. A PROCESS EMBRACES THE INPUTS AND THE OUTPUTS

In practical terms, for example, a process takes a large quantity of parts and fixing materials and builds a car from them. The added value is assembly, which enables the separate parts and materials to be utilised in a way that would be impossible for each of the parts on its own.

In the business or organisational context, there are numerous processes. There are invoicing processes, for example, which add value by calculating what a customer needs to pay and making appropriate demands. There are also more sophisticated processes which may incorporate a wide range of functions and activities. For instance, a commercial process may include the steps it takes to set up and secure trading channels – avenues through which you can sell your products or services. It may include the development of agents who are employed to keep these channels open and to make sales through them. It may also include the exploration of alternative channels and an evaluation of their potential for investment.

We can already see that our definition of a process does not allow us easily to describe the size and scope of the 'average' process. This leads to a consideration of what processes are for. Why should we wish to describe our organisation or activities in this way? To answer this question, let us look at how a process differs from a function.

Processes and functions

Typically, a function has been established to embrace a specialism deemed to be essential to the organisation. It is interesting to see what functions are represented within any board of directors, and to identify the function from which the managing director or chairman has come. Often it is a measure of what the organisation or its stakeholders believe are the most important functions or specialisms. Functional priorities change over time. If finance was key a few years ago, it has subsequently been replaced by engineering or marketing. Interestingly, the personnel or people function is generally less well represented, particularly at chief executive level.

The nature of a function is to ensure that sufficient expertise and the capacity for its application are placed appropriately within the organisation to facilitate achievement of the organisation's goals. The personnel function, for instance, ensures that sufficient knowledge and ability exists on matters of, say, employment law, people policies and practices. The finance function ensures that managers are sufficiently aware of how the organisation's performance is measured in financial terms, and provides a service by keeping a track of the costs and incomes, by investing any surplus funds wisely, and highlighting the financial status of the organisation.

A process, on the other hand, may make use of a variety of functions before it delivers the end-product or service to the customer. The product the customer buys may be well engineered (engineering function); cost-effective (finance and operations functions); made of various materials (purchasing function); put together well, by well trained people (personnel and operations functions); and sold (sales and marketing functions) to meet a particular need of the customer. The customer sees an outcome to which several functions have contributed either directly or indirectly. Our customers do not buy the separate contributions offered by the functions: they buy the *outcome that is delivered through the process.*

The aims of processes

Here lies the clue to the value of seeing our work in process terms. If we analyse our work appropriately, its description in process terms leads us to the customer and to what the customer buys or receives. Or, to put it another way, if we wish to be customer-focused, we can start with what the customer wishes to buy, and work our way back to see what steps and inputs are required along the way. In this manner we can ensure that we only do what we have to do to deliver what the customer wants. Any other actions we take should be challenged. If they do not contribute towards what the customer is buying, what do they contribute to?

By describing what we do in process terms we can readily see the interdependencies upon which our success lies. We can see what our deliverable product is and for whom we are creating it. We can see how and where the functions can best add their respective contributions, and ensure that the transference from one step to the next is kept simple and as direct as possible.

Figure 3

FUNCTION-DOMINATED PRODUCTION

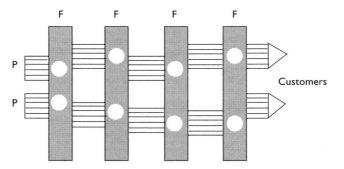

If we see our organisation as only a set of functions, each function is likely to grow and operate on the basis of how its particular specialism develops and of how the functional leader promotes its importance in the organisation. In this way, empires begin to appear and organisations grow in a lop-sided fashion, with insufficient reference to their customers. In Figure 3, the functions are represented by the vertical tubes and the processes as horizontal tubes.

If the functions dominate, they tend to *lock* the processes in such a way that the flow of activities is dictated by the needs and pace of the functions. This can lead to delays and inefficiencies which increase the cost of producing the product or service, and may distract attention from what the customer requires and expects to receive.

If the processes dominate, then the functions follow the lead of the process: see Figure 4. If the process is well designed, efficient and effective, then the functions are utilised at the right time and place to support and enhance the flow of activities to meet what the customer requires and expects.

Figure 4

PROCESS-DOMINATED PRODUCTION.

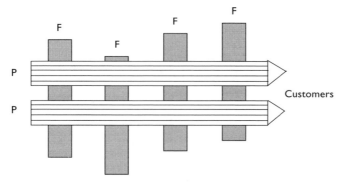

In summary, the aim of the process is to provide us with the most effective, economic and efficient sequence of steps to convert inputs to desired outputs. The aim of the functions, on the other hand, is to provide us with the most effective, economic and efficient specialisms that enable us to take those steps.

An organisation is comprised of both processes and functions. It is the structure, the systems and the practices which balance and integrate functions and processes to achieve stated goals.

If the process's purpose is to create a desired output from certain inputs, we can measure the process overall in terms of whether or not it actually delivered that desired output. In turn, this means that we need to specify the output in clear and measurable terms so that we can assess what we deliver against those criteria.

For example, the goals of a commercial process may be along the following lines:

☐ Find and open two new trading channels in overseas markets by mid-year.

☐ Increase sales of new products to last year's new markets by 15 per cent.

The goals of a production process may be:

☐ Deliver on specification and within costs 100 per cent of the time.

☐ Increase utilisation of capacity by 5 per cent.

The goals of a managerial process may be:

☐ Top-down policy and goal deployment to be completed to all levels within one month.

☐ Performance reviews to be conducted and integrated on a monthly basis at all levels.

These examples indicate that we can be quite specific about the goal of the process in terms of its required outcome. In doing so we recognise that the achievement of these goals may involve more than one function or department. Process goals can be unhelpful, indeed downright confusing, however, if they do not take their lead from the organisation's goals overall. Every organisation needs a guiding direction. Whether or not it is described in terms of mission statements, visions, or simply goals, it supplies the context in which the process operates.

The goals of functions may not have changed much over the years, regardless of the organisation's wider goals – except perhaps in production, where the drum ever beats that much faster. But the processes – precisely because some are concerned with the external world and the potential and actual customers within it – cannot hide behind 'business as usual'. They need to articulate, in their goals and measures, the 'deliverables' which comprise the achievement of the organisation's overall objectives.

So, process goals take part of their form from the organisation's overall direction, but not only from there. The process goals are by implication based on what that process is there to provide, and hence have an internal focus. They also have a degree of precision which reflects the specific requirements of their particular recipients (often a sector of customers).

Figure 5 attempts to put into perspective the three contributors towards the process goals.

Figure 5

SCHEMA OF THE PROCESS GOAL

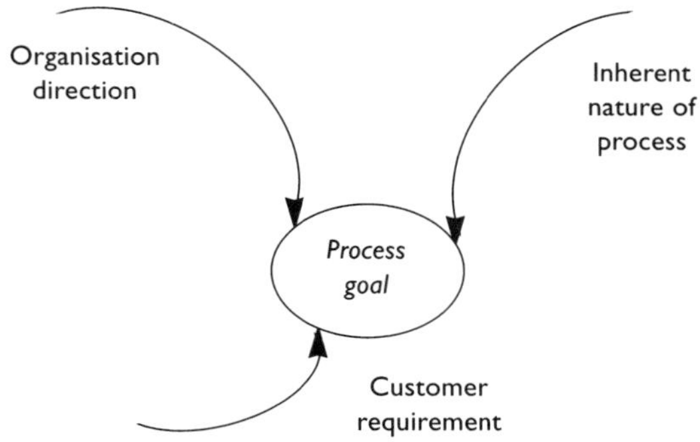

Organisation
direction

Inherent
nature of
process

Process
goal

Customer
requirement

An example is shown in Figure 6.

At their simplest the process goals describe the output of the process – what we want to see delivered at its end-point. If the process is customer-focused, the output will be primarily what the customer expects and wants, to meet his or her requirements.

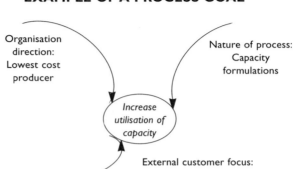

Figure 6

EXAMPLE OF A PROCESS GOAL

Setting the process goals

When establishing process goals we can also look outside the organisation, both for specific goals to aim for and for some sense of the standards which we can apply. Benchmarking can help us here, by providing insights into how other organisations determine their goals, and within what context, and by giving us something to aim for, to stretch for, in order to set achievable yet ambitious standards. In establishing what other organisations have achieved, one can identify features or benefits to single out as potential competitive advantage-points. Others may have ignored a quality your organisation can excel at, so you can design the process to optimise that feature or benefit. For example, the level of interest in turn-around time as a critical customer requirement has meant that those with lean and flexible processes have been able to dominate by means of this particular competitive advantage.

The emphasis may be dictated by the status of the business plan, and hence by the degree to which plans are on track, year-on-year. As long as we are sure that the external situation is truly as we believe it to be, then it may be appropriate to set a goal that reflects the gaps.

In seeking process goals we must resist the temptation to develop several goals per process, so that we end up with too many goals to manage. It is vital to identify the critical few (or even one) and put the effort into achieving so much only.

Measuring the process

Although the goals tell us what to aim at, we still need a means of measuring whether or not we are getting there – and that means we need to know what to measure and how to monitor it.

We all know what is meant by measurement, and yet it is incredibly hard to identify and settle on useful measures. There are many ways to measure things, and we will never succeed if we look for the intrinsic or perfect measure for a given goal or activity. A measure is an aspect of the use we want to make of the item being measured. For example, a pencil can be measured by its length, its breadth, its colour, the hardness of the lead, its current length over its original length, the diameter of the lead and of the pencil, and so on. If our interest in the pencil is over whether it is useful for drawing, then our primary measure is the hardness of the lead, and perhaps its current length. If we want to use it as a rule, or to complete a coloured set, the appropriate measures are different. So it is with measurement of goals, whether they are process or function goals, or indeed organisation-wide goals. We must consider what we are primarily interested in doing with the outcome.

That tends to beg another question – who are we delivering the outcome for? The customers' 'measures' of what we deliver may be quite different from the 'measures' the shareholders use. So in determining the measures we need to take account of all the interested parties and how they will judge performance. It may be that your measures reflect differences and perhaps even conflict. The trick is then to ensure that all can be satisfied (or at least that everyone understands the compromises that have been made)!

A measure, then, is a criterion by which an interested party judges what we deliver, and measurement is what we do to assess performance against that criterion. However, we need to ensure that we apply the 'basket' of measures referred to in our model of performance management in Chapter 1. If you are ill, the doctor takes more than your temperature to determine what is wrong. We need similarly, to identify the least number of measures which collectively inform us, and which cover how the product or service will be judged by the various interested parties.

In terms of measurement of the performance of a process, we should start by measuring what gets delivered at the end of the process, and then work backwards to measure what happens along the way that contributes towards these end-point measures.

If the process is geared to deliver bagged flour to a distribution-point, for example, we can determine the measures by considering what the customers want. The ultimate customers want the flour to be in leak-proof bags, with the right quantity and quality of flour inside. They also want the date to be specified on each bag. The supermarket is the penultimate customer, and the 'goods inwards' person there wants the bags of flour to arrive on pallets, without any corner damage or spillage, and to the correct overall weight.

The distribution fleet is driven by people who want the pallets to be stacked straight, with adequate shrink-wrap, and with clear labels denoting their destination. In addition, they want them to be positioned for ease of loading and delivery.

So far, then, we have various customer requirements to consider. The sort of things we can measure include:

leak-proof bags	date-stamp
quality of flour	quantity of flour in bag
quantity of bags	whether and how palletised
state of the corners	evidence of spillage
how shrink-wrapped	destination labels
drop-off point per load	

If the process goes as far as having the pallets of bags ready to load, then all of these may be legitimate measures. Some potentially overlap – for instance, if we can measure the quantity of flour per bag, we do not need to measure what 100 bags weigh. Some suggest that standards can be set that ensure that measures are met – for instance, standards for numbers of bags per pallet, for a loading sequence onto pallets, and for the application of shrink-wrap, deal with several of the potential issues above. Once the standards are set and communicated, they become the measures by which that step is judged. Here we have moved into measuring the activity, rather than just the output, on the basis of a calculated cause-and-effect relationship between how the activity is done and the status of the output.

If a specification is made for the quality and quantity per bag, of the date-stamp, the label and the number of bags in total, that specification also becomes a scale by which the success of the process – in terms of what it delivers at its end-point – is measured. Measurement starts long before the end-point, however, and should ensure that mistakes are caught early and do not turn up towards the end of the process, needing to be reworked!

How we measure the process depends on what it is supposed to deliver, on the specification that describes critical features and elements of that output, and on any standards set in relation to how it is constructed and prepared for delivery.

Tracking back through the process

If we have set goals that are based on what the customer wants, on what the process can feasibly deliver, and on the direction our organisation wishes to take, we can establish a specification and standards by which we can measure performance as we go towards the desired output. The actual performance against these measures indicates whether we are likely to reach our goal.

Let us take the example of the commercial process goal 'Find and open two new trading channels in overseas markets by mid-year'. The specific outputs from that process are the two new trading channels. What measures can we use to assess our progress?

The customer of the trading channels is effectively the sales department within the organisation – the department requires more potential outlets through which to tempt buyers. Another stakeholder may be overseas agents whose participation in the selling activity is required. Between these two sets of customers their requirements might be:

☐ Poland and Germany as key targets

☐ links with trade associations to be incorporated

☐ positioning within a market likely to buy our products or services

☐ political, economic, and religious aspects to be thoroughly considered and documented

☐ operation of the trading channels to be legal, ethical, and cost-effective

☐ some level of current interest to be evident

☐ key contacts to be vetted, and contracts to be binding.

The process for finding and establishing the two new channels must comprise several steps, one of which is the initial research into potential markets in the countries concerned. Another is getting out there to meet likely people and to create links with the trade associations' local representatives. Yet another is assessing current interest, and calculating what the venture might cost, and for what benefit.

Along the way, the specific requirements of the process customers are initiated and measured against what has been stipulated at the beginning. By specifying what is required as an output we begin not only to set the measures for the process but even to suggest some of the design of the process itself. That is why we need to start at the customer end, to ensure that what we do is actually relevant to the end-point we wish to reach. In this way we ensure that the resources and effort are invested where they can add most value.

In setting up process goals and then the appropriate measures, we inevitably need to consider the design of the process – what was appropriate for last week's output may not be so for this week's, if our customers have altered their requirements. The notion of adding value at each step of the way, is critical for the design of the process, and how it is fulfilled is dictated by the outputs required and the available resources.

But adding value tends to be measured only at specific intervals, not at every step, and we need to decide where the appropriate points are. The essential consideration is to identify what sequence of steps is required actually to add value – at what point is another chunk of value added? Conducting research adds value only when the data is analysed and conclusions drawn. So a sequence of research steps can be measured by the existence of the conclusions that emerge. Getting something typed adds value in respect of the presentation and hence usefulness of a document, but we tend to measure a document by a range of measures of which its typed condition is only one. So the process extends to the development of the data and concepts within the document, as well as its final presentation.

In short, we can track back through a process by starting at the customer end and identifying the sequence of steps which create and deliver a specific output to that customer. It helps to start at the output and define each preceding step, so that we focus only on those steps that are actually relevant to that particular end-product or output. If we start at the input end, we are likely to include all sorts of steps which we have to take but which may make little contribution to the output. We have then to make a judgement on the chunks of steps which comprise that overall process, and which each add a defined element of value.

A familiar process that we can use to illustrate the point is the making of a pot of tea. The output required by the customer is a pot of tea, ready to pour into three available mugs, with sugar and milk at hand for those who want it.

The sequence of steps may be as in Figure 7:

Figure 7

SCHEMATISED PROCESS OF MAKING TEA

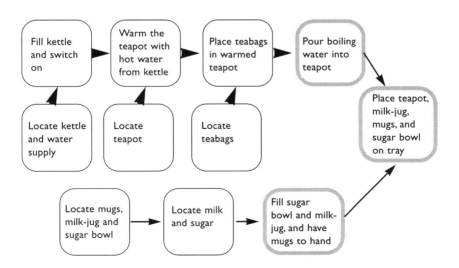

There are three points at which we might measure this overall process:

☐ where the teapot is filled and effectively the tea is made
☐ where the milk-jug and sugar bowl are filled and the mugs are at the ready
☐ and finally, where all come together onto a tray ready for serving.

The process could of course be extended all the way back to taking the customer order or request, and it could include the provision of biscuits or cake and slices of lemon. What the diagram indicates is that there are some things which fit together and which create interim outputs, and therefore which can be measured in terms of those interim outputs. If the customer expresses dissatisfaction, it may be because any one of those interim outputs has failed or because the last step of putting the whole lot together has failed.

By tracking back through the process we can start to see where the chunks are, and therefore what can be measured. To identify the constituent chunks we can consider the final outcome, and decide how it is made up. For example, if the final output is a built conservatory, the constituent chunks might be:

☐ site evaluated and plans agreed
☐ foundations prepared and ready
☐ pre-assembled units arrive
☐ construction.

Each may have quite lengthy processes behind it, and the final outcome works only if these constituent parts have been done well. Failure in any one seriously affects the outcome.

We can conclude that these interim outputs and areas of measurement must tell us what is critical to the end-point success, and hence where the key elements of value are added. Any one of these processes can be tracked back, and it is in doing so that the main chunks may be identified and measured in terms of the interim outputs. So the analysis of activity into the processes and their measurement can be further and further refined to increasing levels of detail. Often the trick is to maintain a sufficiently high-level perspective in order to retain the focus on the critical few elements, and not to get swamped by masses of detail that may quickly blind you to the real issues and opportunities.

This gives us a clue as to how process goals and measures can be translated into department/team/individual objectives and measures. As we move into the actions taken at the most direct level, we must be able to see where and how each contributes to the broader process, for a stated output.

Customer orientation

In regarding our organisation, or our part of it, in process terms we are endeavouring to simplify and optimise the sequences of steps that will deliver the end-products or services to our external customers. We are attempting to position expertise and specialisms within the context of those sequences of steps, and we are seeking measures that enhance our understanding of what contributes most to those outputs which the external customers expect of us. We are left with a focus that is geared towards the customer, and that potentially allows us to respond more quickly to any changes made by the customer.

If we describe our organisation in that way to those who work within it, we enhance their ability to see how and where they contribute to that end-point product or service. If they have an eye on the end-customer and understand what is required there, their efforts to improve can therefore also be focused and inherently reinforcing, as people see the effect of their new contribution.

The notion of continuous improvement has been with us a long time, and has a place in the discussion about processes too. Not only must we look for ways of continuously improving the actions we take within the steps, to improve what they add in value, but we need to review the steps to verify whether they are the best way of achieving the same end-point. We need to watch out for steps that somehow sneak in and become accepted as part of the process, when they were needed only once to meet a special case or because someone did not take an earlier step well enough.

All these can be described as incremental improvements,

mostly well within the remit of those who take the steps. As long as they attune to the current and anticipated needs of the customers, they can be encouraged and reinforced. At every point appropriate measures can be defined, focusing on the end-customer and on the value required to be added at each chunk or stage of the overall process.

But sometimes the incremental improvement makes only a fraction of a difference, and if competition is snapping at our heels, it may not be enough. There are times when a breakthrough may be required.

Breakthrough

The idea of a breakthrough is that it bypasses the current ways and represents a novel and striking route down which to travel to a given end-point. In process terms it usually means that an entire process is called into question. Rather than tinker with the steps within the process, a breakthrough challenges the process itself and suggests a better method. For instance, it could be said that the invention of the Tea's-Maid was a process breakthrough, that xerography was a process breakthrough, that electronic ignition was a process breakthrough, and so on.

When to seek a breakthrough is as much to do with approach as it is with need. You may be well aware that a significant change is required and an obvious solution presents itself, or you may encourage creativity such that a new idea appears and has an immediate application. In most cases a combination of the need and some innovation together result in the breakthrough. But how do we ensure that the breakthrough adds value and does not cause a problem elsewhere?

This brings us back to measures, and in the first instance to the goal of the overall process. If we can start our challenge there and seek to ensure that the goal is still valid, that it has customers waiting for its delivery, and that it is appropriate to our business and to our reputation, we can take that goal as the focus for any idea that may emerge. For example, if the goal is to pay our suppliers within two weeks of their invoices, the breakthrough process may be an electronic data transfer system, cutting out paper cheques, cutting out several authorisations, speeding up the process a hundredfold. We can say goodbye to the cycles of manual and semi-automatic checking and reconciliation, and replace these with a system that focuses the task on the accurate setting up of records and their access rather than on the daily or monthly duties of clerks and managers.

We can measure the success of our breakthrough by seeing whether and how it meets the goal set. Once we are sure that the goal is being met, we can seek out the chunks at which value is added along the way. They are likely to be significantly different from the chunks and their measures of old, and require us to redefine how tasks are measured and how individuals or departments are deemed to operate successfully.

The role of measurement in managing process performance

Just as it is impossible to say how a function has performed without some indicators of what we expected it to do for the organisation, so it is impossible to say how a process has performed without suitable indicators. Part of the difficulty is that we have a sense of what could be expected and some notion of the cause-and-effect links between different aspects of our organisation. Because of this, the temptation is to say after the event that we know what contribution each element made. However, although we may be largely accurate in our intuitive assessment, we need more detail and more specific targeting of the areas of scope if we want our investment of improvement effort to be rewarding.

This is not to advocate *analysis paralysis* but to encourage the identification of a few key measures that tell us whether the process is delivering and whether each chunk is adding the value we want. On that basis, performance assessment can indicate where improvements are needed, or indeed where higher standards of delivery can be formalised and built upon.

Process measurement allows us to reassess the role of the functional specialisms in the creation and delivery of outputs to specified customers. Unless these roles clearly add some value we have to question their existence. In this way, the functional contribution can also be subject to breakthroughs. For instance, the increasing move towards on-line maintenance – a role taken now by the operators rather than the engineers – is a change in the way that engineering adds value. Planned maintenance was a significant shift from the crisis management style that characterised many engineering functions in the past. The whole shift in some organisations of planning the people requirements of the organisation at a strategic level, and hence building in processes for education, training, induction, recruitment and development, changes the focus for the personnel or human resource function, and sets their interventions at levels quite different from those in an organisation which reacts to a current need or crisis. This means different measures for them too. To keep all the functions and organisation processes from spinning off 'doing their own thing' we need common goals and key measures which link each part of the organisation to each other and to the end-customers.

So reviewing a process starts at the customer end, and tracks back through to the supplier end, seeking incremental improvements along the way. It also means that we stand back from the process overall and challenge it for a potential breakthrough. In many senses, the process focus makes review easier, because we should be able to see the connections within the organisation and how they contribute towards the outputs which are the products or services of the business.

In some senses the notion of process is easier to see in a classic manufacturing organisation in which the production process has been around since Ford developed the conveyorbelt method of car production. Even there, however, the notion of process has tended to stop short of a business-wide process. Typically, the production process has been positioned thus:

Whereas in a process organisation, the business process would entail:

Attendant on both these versions are the functions of information systems, personnel, finance, legal, and possibly engineering. In the genuine process organisation they tend to provide an integrated set of services which collectively provide both support and guidance to enable the products to be delivered as promised to the customers.

In the service organisation, a most helpful classification of its elements is given by R. Normann[1], who defines a service organisation as having 'moments of truth' at the customer interface; as having 'service systems' which ensure delivery of the moments of truth time after time; and the 'service concept' which defines what gets delivered to the customer.

The service concept is what gets marketed, and further sequences of action turn that concept into reality and culminate in those moments of truth. If these are what the customer sees, the measures begin there.

To identify some of the processes within your organisation, try out some of the suggested procedures below.

What do I do?
This positions your contribution between your customers and your suppliers, and guides you on the measures that apply within your part of the process.

Draw a sketch of yourself and the customers and suppliers you have. Customers are people to whom you provide specific goods, information, guidance, assistance, and so on. Keep them specific, and do not generalise. Suppliers are people from whom you receive specific goods, information, guidance, assistance, and so on.

Ask yourself,

- ☐ Do my direct customers really want these outputs from me?
- ☐ How do they measure my effectiveness?
- ☐ How do I judge that I have delivered what was needed?
- ☐ What steps do I take to create those specific outputs for my specific customers?
- ☐ Do I use all the inputs I receive?

1 R. Normann, *Service Management: Strategy and Leadership in Service Businesses,* Bognor Regis, Wiley, 1984.

☐ How do I measure the effectiveness of my suppliers?

☐ How do I use these inputs?

☐ How different is my output from the inputs I receive – what value do I add? How do I specify this?

How do I fit in?
This encourages us to look beyond the immediate customers to the end-user customer, and to revise our measures to see whether they obviously contribute towards the end-use of the product or service.

Continue the exploration by means of the questions, keeping an open mind.

☐ What does my direct customer do with my outputs?

☐ Who are the end-users and what do they receive from us?

☐ How does an end-user apply the outputs we deliver?

☐ How does an end-user measure our effectiveness?

☐ How do I add value to that application?

☐ How do my suppliers add value to create the inputs that I need?

☐ How do they assess whether I have what I need?

What opportunities are there for improvement?
This focuses on the steps we take ourselves, and seeks to identify where we currently waste effort or resource, and where improvement opportunities may exist.

Take the outputs you have defined for a specific customer, and specify the steps you take to create that output, including the use of the specific inputs you receive and need to do the task. Be sure to complete your drawing first. Challenge yourself with the following questions:

☐ Where is there duplication of activity?

☐ How many people get involved at any step?

☐ How many sources of input deliver the same or similar things?

☐ How often does reworking occur?

☐ How often do I find that the output was not needed?

☐ How many times does a step or sequence get repeated?

☐ How has the sequence of steps grown over the years?

- [ ] How many steps does it take, and is there a shorter way?
- [ ] Is there an easier way to add the value?
- [ ] If I look at what my direct customer does and my relevant suppliers do, is my involvement necessary?
- [ ] What could be saved or enhanced by taking the improvement steps?

4

DEVELOPING INDIVIDUAL PERFORMANCE MEASURES

Ann Gammie

As Mike Walters indicated in Chapter 2, the linkages between the performance of the organisation and the performance of its individual members are often highly complex. If the organisation is failing to perform to the required standards – in terms of, say, financial performance, quality standards, or customer service – it is always difficult to assess to what extent this can be ascribed to failings in individual performance, and to what extent it reflects broader structural, systems or process problems. On the one hand organisational performance should be more (but is commonly less) than the aggregate of its members' performance. On the other, we should certainly aim to ensure that individual performance accountabilities are as clear as possible.

Accountability

These issues become even more complicated if, as we suggested in Chapter 3, we structure the organisation around the delivery of customer-focused processes. If the process is spread over a number of functions or departments, for example, how do we measure the performance of individuals in each area? In order to begin to understand the links between individual contribution and process or organisational performance, we need to define what is meant in practice by the respective terms *responsibility* and *accountability*. Before we reach for our dictionaries, it is worth saying that there are many different interpretations of these two words (perhaps as many as there are organisations), and that we are less concerned with precise definitions than with understanding some broad but essential concepts. For the purposes of this discussion, therefore, let us propose some simple definitions of the two terms.

If we are *accountable*, we are held to account for particular outcomes – even if not all the activities are under our direct control, or are completed by ourselves alone. So accountability means that we often have to find ways of influencing and persuading others to play their part well and successfully if we are to achieve what is required. In this context it is not sufficient for us to claim, 'But you can't hold me accountable for that – I didn't know it was happening,' or 'But it's not my fault if members of my team don't deliver.' If you are *accountable* for the collective outcome, it is up to you to ensure that the required outcome is produced, no matter who or what else is involved along the way. For example, a government minister might well be held accountable for the actions of his or her department, even though he or she might have little direct control over, say, the actions of more junior civil servants. Similarly, the manager of a process is held accountable for the delivery of its outputs, even though the process itself may pass through a range of functions over which the manager has no direct control.

In considering accountabilities, therefore, we need to be prepared to identify what we can and cannot directly control, and devise methods of securing support and commitment from others for those things that we decide are outside that direct control. How do we ensure that others play their part? What mechanisms do we use to monitor and manage *their* performance? The issues here are likely to be much more about effective communication, co-ordination and persuasion than they are about direction or instruction in the conventional sense.

It is also reasonable for us to hold a particular function *accountable* for its particular role in the wider business or operational process. For example, a business unit head may be held accountable for the timely production and delivery of products to customers, whereas a purchasing function head may be held accountable for the timely provision of high-quality raw materials to factories. In both cases they depend on others for the successful fulfilment of their respective account-ability, and it is up to the respective function head to make sure that all contributors play their parts appropriately.

It is possible, however, that what we do is only part of someone else's accountability – something they have contracted to us to complete on their behalf, because of our expertise, our experience, our resources, our contacts. They would then regard us as *responsible* for that part, and we can expect them to work with us to ensure that we deliver the best outcome for their customer. For example, as part of the purchasing process described above, a lorry driver might be responsible for ensuring that a load of raw materials is deliv-ered from the supplier to the factory by a specified deadline.

In broad terms, therefore, *accountability* implies that we have been charged with delivering a specified outcome, regard-less of whether we have direct control over the various process elements that contribute to the outcome. *Responsibility* refers to those areas in which we have direct control over the deliv-ery of specified output. The two concepts begin to blur when a job-holder has control over all the tasks that deliver an output. He or she is not only accountable to deliver the outputs, but is entirely responsible for doing the tasks that produce them. We tend to describe these situations as areas of *responsibility*.

In an organisation structured around processes, these concepts are a critical aspect of performance management because they cut across the traditional notions of power in the workplace. If we give *accountability* for a process to one person, many others will be *responsible* for completing the constituent elements. As part of the process, functional heads have some expertise in their particular specialisms, and have control over the tasks their functions carry out, and indeed over the people who perform them. However, they generally do not have control over the total process.

In a process organisation, therefore, a business process may be the accountability of one person, but that person has no direct control over several, perhaps most, elements of the process. To take one example, if a marketing person has busi-ness unit accountability – which means that he or she is accountable for the production, sales and delivery of a particu-lar product – then he or she has to persuade and influence colleagues to work collaboratively to ensure that the outputs are delivered and the organisation's goals met. So in the process organisation, the understanding of *power* is different from that which applies in a traditional, functional organisation. Power of authority gives way to influencing power, and control gives way to collaboration.

That shift has a significant impact on how people are measured, and on how we make the links between the performance of individuals and the performance of the organisation. In the process organisation, power is in effect a collective phenomenon. One of the major difficulties faced by organisations moving towards a process orientation is that those who are currently power-holders may not appreciate how much of a shift is required of them!

In developing individual performance measures, then, we have first to determine whether the individual is contributing towards a larger business or operational process. We must consider whether the individual's role involves accountability beyond the personal completion of certain tasks, and beyond the personal areas of expertise or specialism.

Input or output measures

In talking about accountability we made reference to the *outputs* of which a person is expected to ensure delivery. In this context, if we focus on outputs as a means of measuring performance, we are primarily focusing on the needs and expectations of the customer. In other words, we are assuming that, whatever quality, activities or efforts went into the task, the customer will not be satisfied if the expected or promised output is not delivered. And if the customer is not satisfied, there will ultimately be no income to keep us going!

This broad principle applies whether we are talking of internal or of external customers. For this reason, an increasing number of organisations now focus their performance measurement on outputs. The added advantage is that they are often relatively easy to measure, whereas responsibilities or job profiles are far less so. Problems may arise, however, if we focus on inappropriate or incomplete output measures – for example, if we measure volume but not quality.

In some cases there is an argument for measuring people in terms of their inputs – what they bring to the situation. This focus is evident, for example, in the current interest in vocational training and qualifications. It is also evident in the increasingly common organisational requirement for employees to increase flexibility by cross-training – extending the range of skills and knowledge they can apply to the work. Similarly, most approaches to recruitment tend inevitably to be input-focused – we are researching into what that person can bring to the workplace. In the case of very specialist areas of work we may even pay a considerable premium for those skills and talents. Except on a few special occasions, we rarely have an opportunity to measure the outputs that people deliver before we recruit them (although we might use evidence of past achievements as a proxy for this).

Equally, although most traditional approaches to performance-related pay focus on outputs (sales achieved, output produced, and so on), there are an increasing number of pay schemes that have increments aligned to the specific attainment of skills and qualifications. These are particularly common in organisations which are trying to encourage multiskilling or increased role flexibility. In some cases the resulting increments are paid regardless of whether there is an opportunity for that person to apply all that he or she has learned. The competence approach, by which we look for tangible behavioural evidence that the individual can apply the required skill, is one attempt to square this particular circle in areas such as individual development, selection and pay.

My job, my patch, my niche

Vast amounts of effort have gone into defining people's jobs. Millions of hours have been spent clarifying tasks and responsibilities, detailing resources required, reporting relationships, and so on, in an attempt to draw a picture of a complete job. Various job analysis systems have been devised to help us, and their existence is testimony to the difficulty of adequately defining a role or job to everyone's satisfaction, such that performance in the job can readily be measured.

Noting all these efforts, many organisations have become

increasingly aware of the 'white spaces' of the organisation chart – that is, the gaps, boundaries and interactions between jobs – and of the need to manage these effectively if an organisation is to optimise its potential. The great danger of producing precise and tight definitions of jobs and roles is that we inevitably draw a thick and often impenetrable boundary around them. In this way we separate one job from another and create perceptions of barriers between them. In practice, the success of an organisation often lies in people's ability and willingness to manage the spaces between their prescribed roles, ensuring that nothing is left to drop between the islands of responsibilities.

We therefore need to measure individual performance at two levels – in terms of what people do *within* the boundaries of their jobs, and in terms of what they contribute to managing the spaces between their roles and those of others in the organisation. This may mean, for example, that in addition to straightforward output measures (performance against targets, productivity, and so on), we are also looking for defined performance standards in terms of, say, teamworking, collaboration, innovation, or role development. In these areas it is much harder to define quantitative measures of output, so we may instead be seeking evidence of appropriate behaviours, perhaps described as critical incidents ('When have I seen this individual working collaboratively with colleagues?' or 'What examples of innovation have been evident in this person's work?')

In most cases people are assessed and paid on the basis of past performance. The annual review is the typical vehicle for determining whether someone gets a pay rise, a bonus, and/or some recognition for their past efforts. Less commonly, people may be paid for their potential, for their promise, or for taking on a task or role deemed difficult or challenging. For instance, those who take a post to help set up an overseas operation, or to project-manage the installation of new plant, are often paid in line with the anticipated requirements and perceived personal demands. Similarly, parts of the civil service apply a concept called 'job-loading' to reflect particularly high or stressful demands.

The first approach deals in evidence and proof, and the

second deals in potential and belief. Both have their place, but we have to consider the potential impact of each on an employee under review. If we focus on the past, we may fail to encourage employees to develop their potential, or we may discourage them from undertaking risky or demanding roles in case it damages their subsequent performance. If we focus on the future, on the other hand, we are clearly taking a risk that the individual may fail to deliver. We are also potentially implying that we reward people for the nature of their role rather than for their performance in the role. Ultimately, we need to judge which brings greatest benefit to the organisation, and we may wish to 'mix-and-match' these approaches in different parts of the organisation – for example, applying the prospective approach in those areas in which significant development is needed.

Performance today or next year

One of the problems we face in Western culture (particularly in Britain and the United States) is the short time-frame within which we set our thinking and our judgements about performance. Annual reviews of the organisation's performance, and annual reviews of the individual's, force us to assess success within that brief period of one year. In some organisations this period is condensed still further – to six, or even to three months.

In many work situations the potential outcome from an action may take years to manifest itself, and both good and bad effects may roll on for years after that. So what time-scale is appropriate for measuring performance?

It may be deemed sufficient to take performance against a defined milestone and settle for that as evidence that things are progressing in a certain way. But, as often happens, the individual may have moved on before the full impact is felt, and before all the care and attention has been paid to the variables that the originator has identified but no one else has! Commonly, an individual may lay the foundations for results only realised (for good or ill) after his or her departure. The football manager Brian Clough commented when he left Derby County many years ago that he had established a team that would be successful for years to come. The team certainly continued to be successful for some time after that – but how much credit should be ascribed to Clough, and how much to his successor? In these cases what are we measuring?

Conversely, we have all seen examples of the 'larger-than-life' manager who sweeps into a role and creates masses of change, energising people and effecting a turn-around in no time at all. And we have all seen the wake they often leave behind, others having to sweep up the mess and sort out the chaos that has been generated along the way. Often both qualities – the dynamic change-agent and the consolidating sweeper-up – are needed at different points in an organisation's life cycle. But at what point do we measure their performance?

There are no simple answers to these questions, except to say that – as Mike Walters indicated in his discussion of organisational measures in Chapter 2 – no single measure is likely to capture all these variables. In most cases we have to conduct a careful review of the individual's role and the context in which it is carried out. We have to speak to the individual and obtain his or her perspective on the job. And, above all, we must relate the measures to the organisational context – what is it that the organisation wishes to obtain from this individual's contribution, and over what time-scale? Once we have identified these parameters, we can agree appropriate performance goals and measures with the individual. In these circumstances, it is critical that the individual knows, understands and accepts the measures to be applied. Moreover, these measures may change over time. If we are setting targets for a 'change-agent' role, for instance, our targets in the first year might be concerned with how effectively the individual establishes the systems, structures and practices needed to bring change about. It is perhaps only in subsequent years that we start to measure performance in terms of the impact these changes have on, say, business performance.

The message about failure

In the lean and mean organisation, with customer focus, quality processes and just-in-time operations, what scope is there for the maverick, for the truly innovative person?

Innovators are by nature people who have zany ideas, many of which do not get off the drawing board, some of which are tested to destruction, and one or two of which bear fruit. They are therefore people who have to deal with failure and rejection, and who still have to keep up the energy and creativity for the next great idea.

In such cases, what do we measure – especially in an organisation that wants everything 'right first time'? Is the innovator a special case, to whom different rules (and different measures) apply? And if so, where do we draw the line?

Again there are no simple answers. The crucial question is that of organisational context. Does the organisation want innovation and creativity, and if so, how much is it prepared to invest in order to achieve these results? The answers to these questions define the parameters within which innovation is acceptable. All too often organisations either stifle creativity by expecting all employees to work to the same static set of performance standards, or they assume that creativity means throwing away performance management altogether. In practice it certainly *is* possible to measure the performance of creative staff (for example, in new product development) if the focus is placed on outputs – how many ideas should be generated? What proportion should be worthy of further development? What proportion should be capable of being taken forward to market? What is the acceptable level of failure? Within these parameters, development staff can be given the freedom to work and think as they wish. If the output targets are not being met, it is not necessarily an immediate indication of poor performance, but does indicate that the organisation should reconsider its strategy. Are we focusing our attention in the wrong area? Are our targets unrealistic? Do we need to invest more? Or – in the final analysis – is it simply that our development staff are not coming up with the goods?

Measuring individual performance

There was a time when a small group of people would work together to produce an article, and apart from the individuals' keeping a weather eye on how each of the others did his or her bit and on how well the techniques were being picked up, the only measurement was whether the article did what it was supposed to do. Nowadays we seem obsessed with measuring performance from all angles, and we push ourselves into the realms of science to come up with the perfect approach.

The purpose of measuring individual performance is essentially to review individual contribution against organisational needs and objectives. Organisations then tend to use this review in two primary ways (each of which we discuss in more detail elsewhere in this book) with the aim of improving performance. First, the review may be used to provide a basis for payment, on the assumption that a link to pay provides an incentive to maintain or improve performance. Second, the review may be used to help identify continued learning and development needs and opportunities, on the basis that this leads to performance improvement. But these two applications do not always sit together comfortably.

If we know that in order to get more pay we must perform really well, we may be reluctant to highlight the message that we also want to broaden our skills or stretch our abilities. After all, we do not want to indicate that we have current weaknesses, in case this affects our pay review. Equally, we do not want to set demanding improvement targets in case that affects our pay review next year! The danger is therefore that we only go for the incremental addition or stretch target, so that by the time of the next review we are able to show that we performed brilliantly again.

At the same time, we hear increasing talk of 'the learning company' (as we discuss in Chapter 7), and we all believe that continuing personal development is one of the keys to achieving improvements in corporate performance. So what measures should we apply if we want people to feel that learning is not only acceptable but is a vital part of our role within the organisation?

Despite years of effort to separate appraisal from pay, the truth of the matter is that the two *are* connected, and indeed most organisations are comfortable in practice that they should be linked. If we accept this, the measurement of individual performance carries implications in terms of the kinds of behaviour we are prepared to recognise and reward, and in terms of how we value individual contributions.

There is a requirement, then, to align the performance messages with our payment, reward and recognition practices, so that we are reinforcing the same messages. Too often there is a mismatch, and some or all elements of the review and the reward approach become discredited. We stress the importance of innovation and creativity, but we reward people only if they hit performance targets based on our traditional ways of operating. We emphasise quality and customer service, but we reward only those who cut costs or achieve high production targets. We say we want teamworking, but we reward those who achieve individual performance targets at the expense of their colleagues. In all of these cases, far from motivating improved performance, we confuse and demotivate employees.

So how is individual performance measured?

The answer to this question differs depending on whether or not yours is a team-based operation in which rewarding the team is also important. If there is a concept of team in practice, the team will hold *collective accountability* for certain outputs. The achievement of these outputs sensibly triggers recognition and reward, and the measurement is based on the quality and quantity of the output. But how can it be recognised when one or two people in the team contribute more than others?

One school of thought suggests that team pressure manages the poor performers and builds common skills within the team. To take the most radical example, in self-managed work-teams the team decides its own membership and has the facility to elect someone out or in. If we follow this logic through, we should be able to leave the team to sort out the relative contributions made by each person, and indeed leave the team to determine what criteria it uses to measure individual contributions to overall team objectives. Even in less autonomous teams it is arguable that peer pressure helps to overcome problems of unequal contribution.

Another school of thought would argue that it is not sufficient to leave the team to find its own level, and that more direct and positive interventions are needed in order to manage individual performance in the team context. This approach –

which perhaps carries some implications about the extent to which team members are trusted to manage their own performance – would therefore seek to measure both team and individual performance, to ensure fairness of treatment, and to ensure that individuals can be identified as having particular skills or abilities which make them suitable for other roles within the organisation. This latter objective assumes that membership of the team is temporary, and that each individual needs a performance record additional to whatever the team itself is likely to provide.

To measure individual performance we can choose any one of four ways:

☐ the business-focused way
☐ the activity-focused way
☐ the process- and customer-focused way
☐ the person-focused way.

The business-focused way relies on there being a set of business goals and values, which are then translated down through the organisation, becoming more and more detailed and department-specific as they go, until they are converted into individual or team objectives, with time-scales attached. This is described as 'goal deployment' in some organisations, and it depends on a speedy and structured methodology for ensuring that the dissemination is completed thoroughly. As a result, if all the individual and team objectives are added up the goals and values can be recognised. At its least effective (for example, some outmoded management by objective approaches), this approach can collapse into a morass of bureaucracy. Nevertheless, as Mike Walters points out in Chapter 2, we cannot measure individual performance effectively without some understanding of the organisational context. If we do not understand the organisation's needs and objectives, we cannot assess whether the individual's contribution is really delivering benefits to the organisation as a whole.

In the activity-focused way, we measure the activities the individual completes to deliver an outcome – that is, what a person does, day by day and week by week. This method is based on the need for descriptions of jobs according to what responsibilities individuals hold, and hence what tasks they are likely to have to do. There is an inherent assumption that if the person just keeps doing these things, proper and timely results will accrue. The primary risk is that these defined tasks and responsibilities fail to reflect the developing needs of the organisation. A job specification written five years ago may reflect a world (the market-place, the competition, customer needs and expectations) that has been left behind.

If we wish to measure individual performance in a customer-focused way, we must be sure that each person is able to specify who their direct customers are (internal or external), and what precisely they are expected to deliver to each. Then the customer can help set the measurement criteria. Because a process organisation is likely to be customer-focused too, the same point applies. If in doubt, the goals of the process can be translated into the contributions that each person makes to add value along the way. The customer-focused approach provides a precise and tangible basis for assessing performance against arguably the most important criterion of all – are our customers satisfied? Its weakness may be that if it is not conducted against a more strategic understanding of the organisation's needs and goals we may lose sight of the need to develop the level or quality of our activities or to open up new market opportunities. Like those computer companies who provided excellent products and services to mainframe customers but who were unprepared for the shift to personal computers, we may find that although our current customers are overjoyed with the quality of our service we are failing to develop for the future.

A person-focused method of measuring performance relies on being able to assess what skills, knowledge and behaviours someone applies in his/her job situation. Some organisations, for example, have developed competence profiles for specific role or jobs. Again, this can be a useful means of providing clear and accessible performance measures (Is the person demonstrating the specified behaviour? Does the person have the knowledge or skills required to operate effectively?), but may be risky if the defined standards are not aligned with developing organisational needs.

Not surprisingly, given the qualifications set out above, most organisations opt for a mix of these ways of measuring performance. However, they are often not clear about the differences (or indeed the links) between these various approaches, or about why they look at performance from more than one angle.

Individual perceptions

Individuals generally have a view on how well they have performed and use some indicators to assess their own performance. Most people form a shrewd assessment of their contribution, whether or not they share the assessment openly. We discuss some of these appraisal options in more detail in Chapter 5. But it is important to keep in mind what we want individuals to see as a result of having been measured. Do we want them to see performance measurement as a passive step, that they are obliged to undergo, or do we want people to see it as an active step, in which their participation is required and over which they have control of the resulting actions?

As long as we use performance measurement as a weapon with which to beat people or to hold power over them, we are unlikely to allow people to regard it as a tool for themselves, to use as a means of focusing their development and growth. So individual performance measurement needs to be defined firstly in terms of what we want the individual to do and feel as a result. That determines the nature of the approach and gives us some clues on what to measure.

The individual needs to understand and accept the measures as relevant to him or her and as 'felt fair'. People need to see how they personally can affect the measures, and feel that they will be supported to do so. If this means spending time on defining customers and their needs, or translating goals into objectives, then that is what is required.

5

THE APPRAISAL PROCESS

Peter Lawson

My daughter recently defined *learning* for me as 'progressing from where you are to where you are not'. Children progress; they learn rapidly from birth, and are soon able to walk and to talk. As they grow older they are, all the time, learning the basis of new skills which they will develop to a greater or lesser extent over the course of their lives. Learning – making progress from where you are to where you are not – does not end with formal education. Adults, too, may continue to learn, to grow. We may acquire new skills and gain new knowledge. As we discuss in Chapter 7, however, adult learning is more problematic. The learning process itself is complex and varies from individual to individual, and can be further complicated by a range of personal and environmental factors. Individual perceptions about capability, feelings about our own worth and self-esteem, difficulties in accepting the need for change in a rapidly changing world – all these may conspire to stifle individual motivation and enterprise in respect of learning.

Organisations too need to learn – to progress from where they are today to where they need to be tomorrow. The requirement for such progress is a response to a competitive environment that has been transformed through the process of globalisation that has occurred in markets. The emergence of a globally integrated, yet volatile, economic system has placed enormous competitive pressures on many businesses. These pressures are likely to intensify in the coming years as the countries of the former Communist bloc develop their economic capability. All of these pressures require continuous development and continuous learning.

Nor are these pressures limited to the private sector. The public sector today is practically unrecognisable in relation to the public sector of 15 years ago. Privatisation, the Next Steps

Initiative, Compulsory Competitive Tendering, the Local Management of Schools, the Citizens' Charter have all required massive changes in practice and culture. This in turn has involved massive learning.

The performance of an organisation is the application of the sum total of individual learning among its members. This perspective on performance – which underpins the whole of this book – demands that the organisation has a clear idea of where it wants to go and how it is going to get there. Only in this way can we ensure that learning is applied and developed in a manner that enables the organisation to meet its objectives and to move from where it is now to where it needs to be in the future.

How do organisations do this? Typically, it is through their *performance appraisal* processes that they ensure that such learning is applied and developed. This is the point at which corporate objectives are translated into individual performance and improvement goals and measures. This is the point at which we assess how effective individuals are meeting the goals and needs of the organisation.

The important role of such processes in supporting the business objectives of organisations is becoming more widely understood, and organisations are modifying their processes to incorporate this wider understanding.[1] The performance appraisal process may be seen as a key subprocess of the wider performance management process. In many organisations, indeed, the term 'performance management' is used primarily (if not exclusively) to describe the appraisal scheme.

An effective performance appraisal system contains the following elements:

☐ mechanisms to link individual goals and objectives to the overall strategic direction of the organisation through, for example, divisional and functional or process structures (see Chapter 3)

☐ a focus both on objectives and targets (the 'what') and on style and behaviours (the 'how'), so that it is possible to assess not only whether individuals are achieving the

[1] IDS Study No. 576, Incomes Data Services Ltd, April, 1995.

individual targets that have been set, but also whether their performance is in line with the organisation's preferred values and culture

☐ a fully developed and understood administrative process which ensures that performance appraisal is conducted conscientiously, comprehensively, and on time

☐ a cadre of skilled and experienced performance assessors, who are well briefed and supported throughout the process

☐ a formal appraisal forum in which past and future performance issues, and any associated learning requirements, are discussed and agreed

☐ a robust, effective system of quality control which ensures that the integrity of the appraisal process is maintained and that confidence in the process is upheld for all concerned: an important aspect of this is the requirement to evaluate the extent to which objectives and goals set and achieved by individuals have contributed to overall strategic goals and objectives of the organisation.

The performance appraisal *meeting* lies at the heart of the performance appraisal process and is central to the success of the whole process. Considerable skill and sensitivity is required to conduct such meetings in an effective manner, and poor performance at this point is often a key contributor to ineffectiveness in the process as a whole.

At this formal appraisal meeting, the extent to which objectives and goals have been achieved is discussed and agreed, and a consensus is reached between the individual and his or her manager concerning the standard of performance at work. Similarly, future performance requirements are discussed and agreed. Finally, any new learning needed to meet future performance requirements is also discussed and agreed.

The appraisal meeting involves three broad stages.

Stage one: preparation

It is important that arrangements for appraisal meetings are made well in advance so that all concerned have adequate time to make proper preparation. It is also important that these arrangements should be changed only for important reasons:

to rearrange such meetings for trivial reasons demeans both the process and those involved in it. It is important too, at this early stage, to discuss and agree how the meeting will be conducted. A proposed agenda should be outlined.

The next step in preparing for the meeting is for both parties to gather, independently of each other, relevant information such as job descriptions, information concerning previous training and development, any previous performance review documents, information concerning recent performance, and relevant personal data such as health or attendance records.

Both manager and employee should also spend time reflecting upon performance during the period under review and also looking forward to the next period for which new objectives may be required.

A checklist such as the one below may assist in this reflection:

☐ What aspects of the job went well during the period?
☐ What aspects of the employee's performance went particularly well during the period?
☐ What problems were encountered during the period?
☐ How well were these problems dealt with?
☐ Which parts of the job provided most enjoyment?
☐ Which parts of the job were least enjoyed?
☐ The manager may wish to consider the aims and objectives of his or her own role, and how the employee may contribute to them.
☐ Both parties may wish to consider objectives based upon the content of the employee's job.
☐ Both parties will wish to talk about any help and assistance, including training, that may be required.
☐ Both parties may wish to consider any personal aspirations that have been discussed in the past.
☐ Both parties may wish to ponder over any relevant personal, career or professional issues.

Immediately prior to the meeting, the manager should take care to prepare the meeting-place, ensuring that there are no physical barriers to inhibit the discussion. Care should be taken with the positioning of the participants of the meeting. If the individuals are positioned too closely together, it may be perceived as threatening. If they are positioned too far apart, both may be perceived as remote and distant. The manager is the host for the meeting and is responsible for managing the way in which it is conducted.

Stage two: the appraisal meeting

At the start of the meeting the manager should be welcoming, warm and friendly, taking care to put the employee at ease. The manager may open the meeting by reaffirming its purpose, and may also outline the agenda and timing of the meeting. The manager should have ensured that the meeting is not interrupted. If there is any possibility that the agenda will not be completed in the time available, it should be acknowledged and discussed at an early stage, and arrangements agreed for dealing with that situation.

It is suggested that as the meeting develops the manager takes only the brief notes required to summarise and record issues agreed at the meeting. As a rule of thumb the manager should expect to spend 80 per cent of the meeting listening rather than talking. Questioning is an important aspect of the meeting, and the use of open questions should be supported by closed questions only when necessary. As the meeting moves through its agenda it is appropriate for the manager to summarise the content of the meeting. The meeting is all the more effective if the employee feels that his or her point of view has been heard and taken account of. This can be achieved by the manager's reflecting back and/or paraphrasing what the employee has said. The manager should do this in his or her own words. The process may have to be iterative, going round the loop a number of times, until the listener is able to say 'That is exactly right.'

The meeting should end with a full summary of the content of the meeting and of points of agreement and follow-through action.

Stage three: follow-through

All the goodwill created by a well-prepared and skilfully

conducted performance appraisal may be lost by a failure to follow through on actions agreed. Nothing demonstrates a lack of commitment to the process and to the employee involved more graphically. Of course, the employee also has a responsibility to follow through on his or her commitments.

Furthermore, too often the discussion about people's performance at work is restricted to the formal, annual appraisal interview or discussion. The value and impact of this discussion is limited by its very infrequency. Full advantage is gained by making performance an issue for discussion as frequently as possible – perhaps even on a daily basis if it is possible and appropriate.

Dealing with difficult situations

Difficulties do arise during the performance appraisal process. They may arise for any of a number of reasons including:

- [ ] unwillingness to fully engage in the appraisal process
- [ ] inappropriate behaviour by either manager or employee
- [ ] insufficient preparation by either the manager or the employee
- [ ] poor or inappropriate performance, which needs to be addressed in the appraisal process.

When confronting a difficult situation it is necessary to prepare carefully. The first step is to define the behaviour that is unacceptable. Be specific and record precise details of the behaviour, such as how frequently it occurs and who is affected by it. How does it prevent others from achieving their goals?

The second step is to try to understand the possible causes of the behaviour that you have recorded. Carefully observe how the person gets on with other people and the specific result of the behaviour in the work situation. If there are no adverse work outcomes, it is probably best that such behaviour is ignored.

The third step is to prepare to speak with the individual concerned. Before you do this make sure that you are able to articulate and understand any particular feelings that the behaviour arouses in yourself. Try to anticipate any difficulties that may arise during the discussion, and think through in advance how you will handle each eventuality. Try to be prepared for any situation you can imagine. Establish exactly what you wish to achieve through the discussion, and make certain that your arrangements will ensure that you have the privacy and the time to fully discuss the situation.

When meeting the person, quietly and calmly describe to him or her the behaviour that you see. 'This is what I saw,' or 'This is what I heard.' Describe the impact of his or her actions or words on others. Be specific. Do not offer opinions or judgements on his or her behaviour. Ask questions to check understanding. Tell him or her clearly about the change you are seeking, but be flexible and open to any suitable alternative solutions offered. Be prepared to listen to the other person's ideas.

In such a difficult situation as this you will need to remain calm, be firm, believe in yourself and your ability, and have confidence in your position. Use the skills of paraphrasing, feedback, listening. Be assertive in showing concern for yourself, for the person with whom you are dealing, and for anybody else affected by the situation.

Your objective must be to seek an action plan which if implemented meets the needs of all concerned. Obtain specific agreement on actions; agree deadlines for these actions; ensure that you have confirmation that the other person will do what has been agreed upon. Make sure that you follow through and monitor that the action agreed has been taken. Be sure to recognise any change or progress that has been made. Re-evaluate and revise the action as required. If no change arises from the implementation of the action plan, repeat the whole process until the required change is effected.

Ensuring the quality of the appraisal process.

The fundamental purpose of a performance appraisal process is to deliver for the organisation those levels of performance that ensure that the organisation reaches all its goals and objectives. It is therefore critical that managers have the skills and confidence to operate the process effectively. Clearly, the first priority is to ensure that managers are appropriately trained in the arts of goal-setting and performance assessment. Key issues here are likely to include:

☐ ensuring that managers have a comprehensive understanding of the organisation's performance needs and objectives, and of the implications of these for their own functions and departments

☐ supporting managers to develop appropriate quantitative and qualitative measures of performance, as well as suitable personal and performance development goals for their staff

☐ providing managers with the skills and tools to assess the achievement of staff against these defined goals and measures

☐ giving managers the competencies and confidence required to handle the performance appraisal meeting effectively

☐ helping managers to support and motivate staff, on a day-to-day basis, in working towards their performance and development targets.

It is not enough, however, to train managers on a one-off basis, and then leave them and the performance appraisal process to their fate. If this happens, the process almost certainly falls into disrepute: the process loses its credibility in the eyes of those who are delivering performance improvement for the organisation. The performance appraisal process needs to be constantly monitored to ensure both that it is effectively managed and that it continues to meet the needs of the organisation.

Above all, if the credibility of the process is to be maintained, performance assessment must be (and must be *seen* to be) fair and consistent. Personal bias, prejudice, or plain idiosyncrasy must not be allowed to cloud the judgement of managers and to distort their assessment of individual performance. Managers may themselves be poorly motivated or they may think they know it all. They may be overly rigid in their views and assessments. They may oversimplify complicated situations and issues. They may apply stereotypes or trivialise difficulties. They may use inappropriate or misleading language to describe or report individual performance. These potential performance assessment problems may manifest themselves in any of a number of ways:

☐ failure to use the extremes of the assessment scale when appropriate

☐ a tendency to rate nearly all employees as average

☐ overrating or underrating an individual's overall performance because he or she possesses one particularly strong
or weak characteristic

☐ a tendency to be influenced strongly by an employee's
recent behaviour rather than taking into account his or her
performance over the whole period in question

☐ a tendency in assessors to rate other people in the same way
that they perceive themselves, or to overvalue their own
particular strengths

☐ a tendency for performance assessment to drift upwards
over a period of time: this is a relatively common phenomenon, particularly where past ratings have been subject to
challenge or appeal

☐ a tendency in managers to allow their performance assessment to be overly influenced by their own personal values
and beliefs: this might be a particular problem where a
manager's personal values are not aligned with the needs or
objectives of the wider organisation – if, for example, the
organisation is seeking innovation but the manager's
assessment discourages risk-taking.

In response to this kind of problem, more and more organisations are now collecting and monitoring quality control data to
ensure the integrity of their performance appraisal processes
over time. The sort of data collected and reviewed may include:

☐ the proportion of individuals assessed at the various performance levels

☐ the relative proportions of individual and team objectives

☐ the number and nature of objectives and measures set, and
the mix of qualitative and quantitative measures

☐ the distribution of performance assessment in relation to
age, gender, race, disability, length of time in the job, length
in the company, and so on

☐ the timeliness of performance reviews

☐ perceptions of the effectiveness, value and fairness of
performance reviews among employees

Various responses may be appropriate to deal with situations arising from the above. Further training may be required to deal with perceived assessment biases. If managers are setting inappropriate or unclear objectives, there may be a need for better communication of the organisation's needs and goals. A useful discipline in helping to maintain the integrity of performance appraisal processes is to ensure that all assessments are vetted by a third party. It is common for the appraisal process to be assessed, on an individual level, by the appraiser's manager, and, on a collective level, by some central monitoring function such as the HR department. The first assessment helps ensure the accuracy and fairness of the specific performance review, and the second helps to identify any more widespread issues (such as a tendency towards 'ratings drift') which might not be evident to an individual manager.

The linking of money with a performance appraisal process must be approached with great care. In particular it is important to ensure that the introduction of a financial implication to performance assessment does not overshadow the primary purpose of the performance appraisal process – namely to improve performance. The most common problem in this respect is that because individuals are conscious that the performance rating will affect their remuneration, they become reluctant to discuss (or even admit to) any performance weaknesses. Because these weaknesses are not addressed, performance is not improved. Equally, some appraising managers may be unwilling to highlight performance failings in their employees if they are aware that such failings will adversely affect the employees' pay.

The received wisdom, therefore, is that as far as possible the *developmental* aspects of performance appraisal should be kept separate from any assessment for payment purposes. Some organisations separate the two processes in time, so that the development appraisal is carried out at, say, the mid-point in the year, and the pay rating is carried out at the year end. This is a partial solution to the problem, and may at least help to create some psychological space in which the discussion of performance can take place. In practice, though, there is no easy answer. Performance-related pay is, by definition, based on some assessment of performance. No matter how or when this assessment is carried out, it is hypocritical to pretend that it is not to some degree linked to the more broadly focused appraisal process. It is probably better for managers to be open about this linkage, while also emphasising that the two elements do have a distinct purpose and focus. Above all, as we have stressed throughout this book, it is important to ensure that the overall process of performance management is aligned with the needs and objectives of the organisation. If it is not, such weaknesses can only be exacerbated by linking the performance management process to pay.

Similar consideration is required before we allow the data gathered through the performance appraisal process to be used as part of a disciplinary process. Not only does such an approach potentially damage the appraisal process's ability to deliver performance improvement but also care must be taken to ensure that such action does not infringe the employment contract. Moreover, as we have emphasised repeatedly in this book, performance management should not be primarily a punitive process. In general the aim should be to support future performance rather than to punish past failings. If poor performance is occurring, the first step should be to examine all the possible causes and responses, disciplinary action being applied only as a last resort.

360-degree appraisal

In conclusion it is worth highlighting one particular development which an increasing number of organisations are applying as a potential solution to many of the problems and challenges discussed above. Traditional approaches to performance appraisal suggests that only the boss is able to make judgements about and assessments of a subordinate's performance. In practice, though, the boss is often the *least* qualified person to assess some key aspects of the individual's performance. How effectively, for example, can the boss make judgements about the appraisee's handling of his or her own subordinates? How well can the boss evaluate the appraisee's relationship with his or her colleagues and peers, or the appraisee's dealings with customers? In the process-based organisation (discussed by Ann Gammie in Chapters 3 and 4), how well placed is the boss to review the employee's contribution to a process that may cross a number of functions?

In response to these challenges, many organisations are developing tools designed to enable all key stakeholders to contribute to an individual's performance appraisal. This process is sometimes called '360-degree performance feedback'. The stakeholders may include the boss, other relevant managers, direct and indirect reports, peers, and also customers both internal and external. In a simpler form (sometimes called 'upwards feedback') it may involve merely collecting data from the individual's subordinates. This latter approach may be particularly useful when an organisation wishes to develop aspects of, say, teamworking or management style.

In most cases, such feedback is collected systematically through formally constructed questionnaires. If the process is to be effective, the process must display a number of characteristics. First, it must be kept simple. In most organisations, it is unreasonable to expect individuals to make complicated or lengthy contributions to the appraisal of the numerous individuals with whom they come into contact. In most cases, therefore, participants should be required only to complete a simple multiple-choice questionnaire. Second, it is critical that feedback information is collected anonymously, with guaranteed confidentiality for the participants. Without such a guarantee most of us would find it hard to comment honestly about, say, our colleagues or our boss. Third, it is essential that the process is constructed to encourage constructive feedback. Questionnaires should, for example, be designed to help identify improvement opportunities rather than simply to criticise past failings, and should help to highlight strengths as well as weaknesses.

It is argued that 360-degree appraisal provides a comprehensive indication of how successful an individual is in the *totality* of his or her relationships at work. The receipt of such comprehensive feedback can be a very powerful experience and often engenders behaviour change in the individuals concerned. Although it may be possible for us to challenge or resist the judgement of a single individual, it is much more difficult to reject a collective and widely held view. The power of the feedback lies in fullness and in its balance, and also in the fact it arises from people with whom the individual works closely on a daily basis.

It should be noted, however, that it is different in character from more conventional performance appraisal processes. In particular, 360-degree feedback tends to focus primarily on the development of the skills and competencies which organisations believe will improve organisational performance, rather than on the business goals and objectives that have been cascaded down, through and across the organisation. The simple questionnaire format, for example, does not easily allow us to explore complex issues of individual performance against targets – particularly as many of those responding may, at best, have, only a limited understanding of the standards or targets that have been set for the individual. External customers, for example, will have views about how well they have been treated by the individual, but can have little or no awareness of the performance required from the individual in terms of, say, quality standards, sales targets, business development, and so on. In general, therefore, the organisation will seek qualitative feedback about the extent to which the individual has demonstrated certain defined competencies – flexibility, responsiveness, teamworking, leadership, and so on. The assumption is that if we have identified the competencies that are genuinely central to the organisation's performance needs, demonstration of these competencies constitutes effective performance.

This in turn, however, implies that 360-degree feedback processes should be constructed with some care. If we have failed to identify the appropriate competencies, or if we give insufficient thought to how we weight the various contributions, we may find that we are failing to develop the types of performance that the organisation requires. For example, if we give undue emphasis to feedback from external customers (important as this undoubtedly is), we may be undervaluing critical aspects of internal performance, such as future business development. In many organisations it may be appropriate to adopt a dual approach in which 360-degree feedback is parallelled by a more conventional top-down form of appraisal which addresses the individual's performance against organisationally-driven standards and targets. We suggested earlier in the chapter that performance appraisal needs to address both *what* we do and *how* we do it. In our ideal model of appraisal, the 'what' may be reviewed through a more conventional target-/standard-based assessment process, whereas the 'how' (that is, the extent to which we display the behaviours and competencies needed by the organisation) is most effectively evaluated by seeking contributions from all those with whom we interact.

6

PERSONAL DEVELOPMENT PLANNING

Mairin Gannon

Increasingly, organisations are stressing the need for employees to take responsibility for planning their own personal development. There are numerous reasons for this growing interest in personal development. In organisations in which there is an emphasis on reducing headcount, it is critical that the remaining staff remain motivated and empowered to deliver stretching objectives. In organisations facing dramatic change, employees often have the best understanding of the development they need to deliver the organisation's objectives. In organisations that are de-layering, traditional career paths are perceived as ebbing away, and employees need a process that encourages them to think of new models of development to enhance their skills and ability to deliver to the organisation. Above all, many organisations are seeking to create a culture in which people have an interest in and ownership of their own learning and development.

Many organisations are assisting staff to do this by encouraging them to focus on the notion of 'optimal fit'. The assumption is that to deliver an optimum performance, an individual needs to have the skills required to deliver the role, to gain job satisfaction from his or her contribution, and to feel committed to the tasks.

Against this background, in this chapter we focus on a structured personal development planning process to ensure that individuals

□ avoid putting all their eggs in one basket
□ stay flexible and responsive to the needs of the organisation

☐ retain the ability to grow in the current job by concentrating on 'optimal fit'.

The starting point for this process is the production of a skills checklist, listing those key skills vital for the organisation to retain and develop in order to compete in tomorrow's markets. The process itself is in three clear phases:

☐ 'fit' in the current role
☐ looking forward and goal setting
☐ development planning.

Stage one: determining 'fit' within the current role

The first stage of any personal development process is to obtain an accurate understanding of where the individual is *now*. In organisations in which there is no comprehensive appraisal system, this may in effect mean starting from first principles. Even where the organisation has an appraisal scheme, it is likely only to be a starting point.

In order to plan our development accurately, we need to think more widely about our roles in the company. This means that we need to take a check on our *interests and values*, as well as our skills, to ensure that we are currently performing to the best of our ability and achieving optimal fit with the organisation's needs.

Because our job satisfaction and our commitment affect how well we do our job, we need to seek to develop in these areas.

Figure 8

ELEMENTS OF A ROLE IN A COMPANY

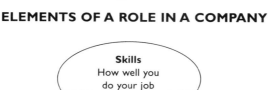

In Chapter 5 we extolled the virtues of 360-degree feedback, and such feedback is a useful starting-point for *skills* assessment. We use skills in everything we do, both at home and in the workplace, and to operate at a higher level of performance we need to utilise all our skills to their greatest possible extent.

Starting to identify current skills

In assessing current skills, a good place to start is to identify three or more major accomplishments in recent years. Accomplishments may be work-related, or related to activities outside the workplace, although it is helpful if there is a balance towards the former.

Using the prepared skills checklist, it is possible to assess which skills were used in these accomplishments, and which were not. Those skills that occur many times could be said to be a subset of the individual's 'transferable skills' – those skills that we carry around and apply in all jobs and situations. For many individuals this exercise highlights skills that they did not know existed or realise that they possessed. Furthermore, the exercises focuses the individual on 'what it was that I did' during the course of that accomplishment, not on the 'areas I am expected to know about', therefore mirroring the shift to competency development apparent in many industries today. The more accomplishments an individual examines, the more concrete the list becomes.

However, listing out transferable skills tells us nothing about what is required for the current role. It is here that the interplay between the views of the individual and those of the line manager adds real value.

Identifying critical skills for the job

The process by which this interplay happens varies, but generally the process should comprise the following elements. First, using the skills checklist referred to earlier, the individual should rate each skill according to

☐ the degree to which this skill is applicable in the individual's current role

☐ the level of proficiency that the individual currently demonstrates.

This process should then be carried out simultaneously by the line manager on the individual and the results compared. Generally this process stimulates useful debate, particularly where there is a wide divergence of results. It forces individual and manager to refer back to, and to prioritise, objectives that have been set, and to reassess what is required to deliver them.

The process also stimulates debate about how required skills or competencies may change in the future to meet changing demands on the business. The objective of the exercise is to come to a consensus about those skills that are essential to the current role, and also the extent to which the individual demonstrates these key skills. By doing this the individual can identify the greatest gaps between the *importance* of the skill and *performance* of the skill. This in turn indicates *priorities for development*.

Identifying strengths and development areas

It is important for the individual to understand that skills are not just a list of general abilities or areas of expertise. Skills are important assets to the individual and the company. They are the currency that individuals use to succeed at what they do.

Knowing what skills we possess allows us to build on our strengths. Targeting development areas allows us to develop for the future. It is critical therefore that individuals can accurately assess their strengths and areas for development. In order to distinguish these, individuals need to use a process that integrates ability to perform with preference of use.

Using the organisation's skill checklist and line manager's feedback, individuals should categorise the list of skills into one of four categories:

☐ perform well and prefer using
☐ perform well but do not prefer using
☐ do not perform well but prefer using
☐ do not perform well and do not prefer using.

In this way the individual now has an inventory of skills made up of:

Figure 9

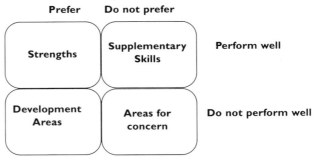

SKILLS INVENTORY

Clearly, the implication for an individual's development in both current and future roles is to structure activities to make best use of those skills an individual has placed in the first quadrant. But of course this is not always possible, and we need therefore to turn our attention to the other three quadrants.

Quadrant two contains those skills which are, perhaps, so well used that their use no longer give us pleasure. These have become what we might politely term 'innate' skills. If the current role requires that these skills form an important part of the job, there may be an implication that the individual is suffering from 'role fatigue'. Future development may require either that some of these skills are 'de-emphasised' in the current role, or that the individual is moved into a new role.

Quadrant three contains those skills which are good prospects for development. Incorporating them into an individual's job will provide an element of challenge and satisfaction.

Quadrant four represents those skills which, in an ideal world, we would drop from our job or delegate to others. Whereas quadrant one's skills – our strengths – allow us to be known as being successful in what we do, quadrant four's skills are those that get us a bad name. An individual ought to ask a few searching questions when examining skills listed in quadrant four.

☐ It possible to change current responsibilities so I am required to use less of these skills? (If so, do it!)

- □ If some of these skills are required in the job, and will continue to be required in the job, should they be priorities for development? (Clearly, yes!)
- □ If a lot of these skills are required in my current job, am I in the right job? (Possibly not!)

This last question provides the focus for the next section of the chapter, in which we will examine *interests* as a focus for development. At this point, however, let us summarise the information that an individual has collected thus far.

Firstly, using a self-generated list of work-related and non-work-related accomplishments the individual has generated a list of skills and competencies that he or she uses regularly to achieve success in different areas. These can also be termed *transferable skills*. This exercise is particularly important in organisations with no real history of assisting employees to manage their development.

Secondly, with the help of the line manager, the individual has determined what skills are *important to perform* to achieve set objectives, and the *extent* to which the individual currently performs these skills. The output from this exercise focuses attention on the priorities for development in the current role.

Thirdly, the individual has categorised skills into one of four sections, depending on both his or her performance of the skill and the extent to which he or she likes using that skill. The output from this exercise is an inventory of

- □ strengths
- □ areas for development
- □ supplementary skills
- □ priorities for action

which takes the individual beyond the current role.

As we noted earlier, although skill identification and development is important to ensure success in current and future roles, attention also needs to focus on those elements that provide us with job satisfaction and a sense of commitment – in other words, ensuring that our *interests* and *values* are met within the job.

Interests

As we grow, we are often asked the question, 'What do you want to be when you grow up?' In my childhood, astronauts were popular; nurses, doctors and teachers even more so. We are often drawn to occupations that appear prestigious, and, later, to those that pay reasonably well. We rarely have an understanding of the tasks that need to be carried out on a daily basis to be successful in the job. If we asked children what they wanted to *do* when they grew up, we might elicit a set of answers very different from previous ones.

In my work with companies, I come across many individuals who find it very difficult to describe or assess the level of job satisfaction that they get from their jobs. Some individuals have a vague sense of unease, a sense that all is not well with their job, that it could be more satisfying. Others are more direct: 'Parts of my job bore me rigid.' Part of personal development planning is about assisting individuals to identify where their interests truly lie, and seeking to incorporate more of these interests into their roles to increase job satisfaction, thereby enhancing performance.

There are many questionnaire-type tools on the market to assist individuals to do this. Most tools categorise interests in themes, as does the following, which comes from the work of John Holland, a well-respected authority in the field of linking interests to jobs.

Realistic – athletic or mechanical; prefers to work with tools, machines, objects; likes to tinker with and fix things

Investigative – observing and learning, analysing, evaluating and solving problems; interested in the physical sciences

Artistic – intuitive and innovative; like to be free to use imagination and creativity

Social – enlightening, informing and training, good communicator who likes to work with other people

Enterprising – likes to work with others through influencing persuading and managing towards goals; enjoys leadership role

Conventional – enjoys working with data and numbers; likes structured environments and following through

John Holland argues that by analysing our interests in this way we can match our interests to those interests demanded by different jobs.

I often ask managers in the companies I visit to complete a questionnaire to determine their interest profile. When we look at a typical interest profile of an manager in a technical or scientific organisation, we often find a combination of realistic and investigative interests featuring very strongly. When we profile the job of a manager, however, the interests that the job demands are a combination of the social and the enterprising. For some managers, therefore, the job of a manager may not provide a huge amount of job satisfaction, and indeed the role of technical expert may be a more appropriate career path than a management career path.

A second route by which to examine interests is to go back to the exercise which looked at an individual's preference for using different types of skills, and to look for themes emerging from preferred skills and non-preferred skills that match the themes in the six interest areas outlined above.

Once individuals have assessed and confirmed their interests, they are in a position to develop areas of their job that will enhance job satisfaction and therefore contribution. In addition, this work assists individuals to seek out future roles they might play which provide a good match for their skills and interests.

Values

The final part of ensuring optimal fit involves considering the extent to which an individual's current values are met in the current role, and how they might best be met in future roles.

As developers of people, we often gloss over the question of values. This is a dangerous mistake. If you think of the last time that you had difficulties in your role, it is an odds-on bet that the issue was not to do with a lack of skills for the role, or a question of job satisfaction. It almost always arises because of a values conflict inherent in the role and the way it is carried out. The majority of individuals who seek career counselling do so because of a difficulty in one of five value areas:

Relationships – who you work with and how you prefer to interact

Supervision – how you prefer to be supervised

Recognition – how you prefer to be acknowledged for a job well done

Challenge – the extent to which you enjoy work that is changing or new

Development – the opportunity that the role presents to develop skills and knowledge

An important part of personal development is for an individual to question his or her values in the above areas, and determine the extent to which these values are satisfied in the current role.

If some or all of an individual's preferred values are not met in the current role, commitment to the job will be adversely affected through increased stress and lack of fulfilment. The result of this is significantly reduced potential to deliver an excellent performance.

In practice, this area is very often glossed over because it is a difficult area to discuss between individual and line manager. Where there is no clear focus on values as part of personal development planning, value conflicts are not recognised for what they are, and are lost behind discussions about skills and objectives. Because of this, by distinguishing values as an important part of development planning, we can enable individuals to bring to the table recommendations in

☐ seeking assignments which involve working with others more closely

☐ training in teambuilding to improve relationships at work

☐ offers of help with supervision

☐ taking of clear authority and accountability

☐ suggestions of project checkpoints to allow easier supervision and meeting of expectations

☐ giving and receiving more regular structured feedback

☐ realistic identification of promotion opportunities

☐ attention to specific performance criteria to facilitate recognition

☐ specific proposals to broaden the role

☐ ideas for added value project development or job/task rotation

- consideration of a range of development tools to widen the skill base.

Guidelines for a successful initial planning meeting

At this point in the planning process, an individual has a wealth of knowledge about his or her fit in the current role. The next step is to share this knowledge with the line supervisor to check its accuracy and value. A good guideline for individuals and line managers to follow during this discussion are the following 11 steps.

- Ensure that all of the work done to date is easily accessible, understandable, and summarised.
- Begin the discussion by sharing an accomplishment from the past year that you both feel good about.
- Re-establish those skills you both perceive as strengths, and clarify what you were thinking when you both rated them this way.
- Identify those skills you both perceive as development areas.
- Clarify why you feel that way, and why they are prioritised in the way that they are.
- Discuss what you like doing, and want to do more of, in relation to your strengths.
- Discuss your development needs including the areas you *would like* to develop, and which areas you *need* to develop.
- Clarify differing perceptions.
- Discuss interests and fit in your current job, including ways to create a better fit.
- Discuss values and fit in your current job, including ways to create a better fit in the current role.
- Summarise agreements and conclusions, clarify roles and responsibilities for next steps, and schedule a follow-up discussion.

At this stage, the individual has a list of action steps relating to the current role and is now ready to look at goal-setting for the future.

Stage two: looking forward and goal-setting

Like the first stage of development planning, the second stage should be worked through in a structured fashion in order to gain value from completing the process, and to ensure that goals set are rooted in reality.

There are three clear activities within the second stage of personal development planning:

☐ understanding the needs of the organisation
☐ understanding the development options available to the individual
☐ setting development goals.

Understanding the needs of the organisation

Even those individuals who plan their development (and there are surprisingly few of them around!) often do so in a vacuum, having failed to recognise the importance of an accurate assessment of the challenges and trends their industry and company is facing, and the implications for them as individuals. Identifying personal development actions that are compatible with individual needs is not enough. The future needs and priorities of the organisation must be taken into consideration for that plan to stand any chance of gaining support and being successful.

Unfortunately, many individuals are not skilled in garnering the formal and informal sources of information in order to make realistic development choices. Many companies insist that individuals take more responsibility for their own development, yet fail their employees by denying them access to the information that they need to take this responsibility.

The best source of information has traditionally been – and continues to be – people and networks. Organisations who are looking seriously at encouraging individuals to take responsibility for their own development, whether as part of the current 'change' process, or as a separate initiative, choose to do this by facilitating cross-functional workshops aimed at sharing information about

☐ trends within the industry
☐ challenges facing the organisation

- [ ] current business issues
- [ ] implications for the development of human resources within the company.

These discussions need to be supplemented by more formal sources of information, such as public affairs bulletins, annual reports, press releases, strategic planning documents, and careful and thoughtful use of such processes as team briefings. Gathering this type of information and verifying conclusions with supervisors, departmental heads, and other senior managers will provide an individual with a backdrop against which to consider the type of options available for goal-setting.

Considering options for development
The options that make the most sense for an individual are best determined by the process of self-analysis and resulting understanding gained from the first stage of the personal development planning process, together with an accurate assessment of organisational realities and needs gained from the second stage.

Furthermore, if you consider what sort of things people say when asked to define success at work –

- [ ] getting recognition for a job well done
- [ ] increasing challenge and responsibility
- [ ] working with other divisions and companies
- [ ] learning new skills
- [ ] applying all the skills I possess
- [ ] feeling I am making a contribution
- [ ] respect from peers
- [ ] seeing projects through to completion
- [ ] working on new technology
- [ ] moving up the management or technical ladder

– you will see that only the last of these requires promotion. All of the others can be achieved by a combination of other options:

- [ ] improving performance in the current role
- [ ] working towards future changes in the current role

- ☐ enriching the current job
- ☐ moving sideways within the organisation
- ☐ moving down within the organisation
- ☐ moving out of the organisation
- ☐ continuing to explore opportunities for development.

Against the backdrop that knowledge gathering has created for the individual, and considering the inescapable fact that downsizing and de-layering often reduce the option of continuing to progress 'up' the career ladder, an individual may now be forced to seriously consider the remaining seven options for development.

Improving performance
Improving performance is likely to be a realistic option for individuals if:

- ☐ individuals are able to identify that there are training and development opportunities available, and time is available to invest in development
- ☐ their performance reviews suggest ways of improving in the current role
- ☐ there is a culture of doing the best job possible within the company
- ☐ performance feedback is regular and valued.

This option might involve an individual in

- ☐ increasing the frequency of performance reviews
- ☐ identifying a training course
- ☐ looking for ways of working more effectively, saving time and effort
- ☐ shadowing those in similar jobs
- ☐ experimenting with new techniques
- ☐ letting others know that he/she is committed to excellence.

Working towards future changes in the current role
This is a realistic option for development if:

- ☐ there is an understanding of different requirements from the department in future

- □ the organisation encourages innovation
- □ the future, and how to prepare for it, is often discussed
- □ good performance is often recognised through increased job responsibility.

Taking this option might involve an individual in

- □ talking specifically with the line manager and team members about what they see as new job requirements
- □ ensuring they keep up to date with new technology and work methods that may impact on their job
- □ seeking out clues about the future, such as budget and organisation changes, or changes in personnel
- □ staying flexible through training or other development experiences.

Enriching the current job

This is likely to be an option for individuals if:

- □ there are frequent opportunities within the role to take more responsibility
- □ there are opportunities for working cross-functionally in project teams
- □ the company demonstrates its interest in better utilising the abilities of its staff
- □ there are opportunities to delegate activities to others.

This option might involve individuals in

- □ examining ways to work at tasks they prefer
- □ evaluating how they work, the processes and procedures
- □ scheduling job enrichment discussions with a line manager, and having specific enrichment ideas to present.

Moving across the organisation

This is likely to be an option for individuals if:

- □ other parts of the organisation are growing
- □ the company is open about opportunities across the business
- □ others have successfully made this move in the past.

The individual might

☐ list the other divisions that are of interest and gain knowledge about them
☐ watch for lateral opportunities and indicate interest in them
☐ identify others who have made lateral moves and develop a strategy with their help
☐ network widely.

Moving up within the organisation
This is likely to be an option if:

☐ several others have been promoted recently
☐ the organisation is growing
☐ there are a lot of new recruits.

This option often involves individuals in

☐ identifying which training and development best prepares them for additional responsibility
☐ letting line managers know they are ready for promotion
☐ keeping personal files and CVs up to date
☐ targeting the position that they want, rather than rushing into promotion.

Moving down within the organisation
This is a likely option if:

☐ opportunities do exist within the organisation but at a lower level
☐ peers also feel 'plateaued out'
☐ those individuals who have done this in the past are still seen as contributing to the organisation.

It is likely that individuals will have to

☐ look for parts of the organisation that would be appropriate to move into from a value-added sense
☐ think about how they will structure the message to colleagues
☐ ensure that the downward moves make good sense in terms of enhancing their future potential

☐ prepare for the financial realities of a downward move.

Moving out of the organisation

This is likely to be an option for individuals if:

☐ there are fewer positions within the organisation than there ever were

☐ there are plans to reduce the size of the workforce

☐ substantial groundwork has not identified a suitable position resulting from other options.

Individuals may have to

☐ consider whether the risk is worth taking: will there really be a better 'fit' at other companies?

☐ contact other organisations to determine opportunities

☐ determine whether they are comfortable discussing this with their line manager and agreeing about a time-frame for moving.

Exploring for future positions

Exploring for future positions is an option if individuals are unsure of their plans for the future and unaware of the opportunities that exist within or outside the company. Working on task and project teams or temporary secondments often assists individuals in making this kind of decision.

The above options are merely guidelines. It is important that they are translated into future-oriented specific goals which pull together all the development work an individual has done to date. Identified goals need to be clear, realistic, specific, and reachable. They also need to be consistent with an individual's self-knowledge about skills, interests, and values, and also with the goals of the organisation. They should generate action and enthusiasm, and include information on the what, when and why.

Stage three: development planning

Development planning should take account of

☐ specific actions to develop in the current role

☐ specific actions to develop in future roles

☐ priorities within the list of development actions identified.

Action steps

Development for the current role should concentrate on the areas for development identified in the initial planning meeting referred to in Stage One. These areas for development centre on creating a better or optimal fit for skills, interests and values, and the output is a series of action steps.

Development planning for future roles begins with the goals that have been identified as a result of considering the *most likely* options. Some of these goals relate to specific jobs in the future. Others relate to more general areas for future development. It is generally helpful for individuals to spend a considerable amount of time working with these goals, using a process such as force-field analysis to identify and prioritise the action steps necessary to get them.

Prioritising action steps

For most individuals there is a cross-over of action steps relating to both the current role and future goals, particularly where the preferred options for future development have focused on improving performance, working towards future changes in the current role, or enriching the current job.

It is important for individuals to accept that the top-priority action steps are those that relate to both the current job and to future roles, and that the second priority has to be those actions that relate to the current role, which ensures that the individual continues to deliver.

The implication of this is that action steps relating solely to future development may have to be carried out largely in the individual's own time or at a financial cost to the individual. However, the level of support for all actions should be negotiated and agreed with the individual's line manager before a draft development plan can be written.

Writing the draft development plan

Because the development plan is the plan of action for performance improvement, at the very least it should include information on:

- specific goals
- development areas
- standards for measuring development
- what activities are to be undertaken to meet development needs
- what resources are needed
- immediate actions (first steps)
- time-frames.

The draft plan serves as a blueprint for intention. The first step is to agree this plan with whichever manager the individual is responsible to, and to set specific dates to review progress and update the plan.

7

LEARNING AND DEVELOPMENT

Shirley Dalziel

In the preceding chapters we have discussed the processes by which performance is measured and managed, and the techniques that can be applied to translate corporate performance requirements into individual development goals. However, as Peter Lawson suggested in Chapter 5, if we are to achieve these personal development goals, we need to do so through a process of learning. In this chapter we explore this process in more depth, with the aim of understanding some of the tools and techniques we can apply to improve its ease and effectiveness.

What, then, do we really mean when we say that someone has *learned* something?

One definition is that 'learning is a relatively permanent change in behaviour that occurs as a result of practice or experience' (Bass and Vaughan, 1967). But this commonly accepted definition implies that learning only takes place if some aspect of a person's behaviour changes as a result.

Does this mean that learning has not taken place if someone has an increased understanding about a particular situation but chooses not to behave in a new way? Or that learning has not taken place if there is increased understanding but that the individual has not yet had an opportunity to apply the new behaviour? At work, for example, we may undertake training in, say, the principles of Total Quality but feel that we are not in a position to implement these back in the workplace. And yet, even though our behaviour may not have changed, we may have developed an understanding that will potentially help us to manage or work more effectively in future.

It is not enough, therefore, to define learning only in terms of observable changes in behaviour. We also need to consider changes in attitude and underlying belief. If we accept this broader definition, it raises practical problems about how we assess the success of interventions designed to promote performance improvement through learning. How can we evaluate the effectiveness of a training course if there has been no direct impact on behaviour?

In responding to this question, Pedler and Boydell have suggested that we should distinguish between 'learning' and 'development'. Development, they suggest, is concerned with achieving a different state of being or functioning – including demonstrable changes in behaviour. Learning, on the other hand, is more concerned with achieving an increase in knowledge or a higher degree of an existing skill. In the work context, a training intervention may promote either or both of these objectives, depending on its purpose or focus. We may aim to provide participants with additional skills which they may not necessarily apply immediately. We may aim to influence participants' attitudes and behaviours without necessarily providing new skills or knowledge. Most commonly, perhaps, we aim to do both, by supporting changes in behaviour through the provision of new skills or knowledge. In each case it is important that we understand what we are trying to achieve, so that we can evaluate our performance accordingly.

In this chapter, therefore, we build on Pedler and Boydell's thinking to define *learning* as any new information, awareness or understanding that is incorporated into an individual's mental world, and which may at some time be applied if the appropriate circumstances arise. Dixon (1994) refers to these mental worlds as 'meaning structures', which we create in our interaction with the outside world. When we learn, we adjust this meaning structure, even though this may not be immediately apparent in our behaviour. In other words, when we say that something has been 'learned', we cannot automatically infer that there has been a change in work performance. The practical application of this learning requires further 'development', which may be dependent on a wide variety of factors – the perceived relevance of the learning, external constraints on our behaviour, the expectations or requirements of others, and so on.

How we learn

We can examine theories of how we learn under two main headings: the Behaviourist approach and the Cognitive approach.

The *Behaviourist School* was an early attempt to describe how learning takes place. The earliest, and perhaps best known, experiments in this area were those of Pavlov, in which he conditioned dogs to salivate to the sound of a bell. Salivating is a normal reflex response to food. As soon as the dogs thought food was about to be served, they started to salivate in anticipation. Because the bell was rung just before the food was produced, the dogs came to associate the bell with food and started to salivate. Eventually the response occurred even if no food appeared.

Pavlov's work, although seminal, has relatively little relevance to performance management in the work context. After all, even in the most autocratic organisation, there is generally little need for employees to apply responses such as salivation, knee jerks, eye blinks, or other reflexes!

Skinnerian conditioning, on the other hand, has much more relevance to the work context, even though it too was originally applied to animals. Most of Skinner's work utilised rats and pigeons, and a contraption called a 'Skinner's box'. He found that by rewarding and punishing apparently random behaviour, he was capable of controlling its occurrence. For example, if a hungry rat kept in one of these boxes accidentally brushed against a lever, which delivered a pellet of food whenever it was pressed, the rat very quickly learned to push the lever (the stimulus) frantically to satisfy its need for food (the reward). Skinner found that he was able to control the frequency of behaviour by varying the frequency of reward – by withdrawing it altogether or by delivering of a painful electric shock.

Although few employers have resorted to electric shocks, this approach to learning has been widely applied in working situations, in such areas as payment and reward systems, appraisal schemes, job training and disciplinary procedures. If we are aware, for example, that certain kinds of behaviour lead to specific rewards (such as bonus payments), we tend to act accordingly. Perhaps the most significant application of

Skinner's thinking is the concept of behaviour modification, which was originally used with people with learning disorders, some forms of mental disability, and in the treatment of phobias and other behavioural problems. It builds upon the concept that behaviours that are rewarded are repeated, and those that are punished are avoided. Peter Honey in his book *Solving People Problems* provides numerous examples of this technique in practice.

In the work context, this can be one of the key tools to promote (or, indeed, hinder) changes in organisational culture and values. If we wish to promote quality values, we may choose to reward behaviours that produce high-quality products or that help the organisation to meet its customers' requirements. If we wish to promote innovation, we may choose to reward behaviours that demonstrate creativity or that support the generation of new ideas. Conversely, it is not unusual for organisations to try to introduce new cultural values while continuing to reward behaviours which are no longer required – the 'quality' company which only rewards productivity, or the 'innovative' company which punishes risk-takers, for example.

We addressed some of these issues in more detail in Mike Walters' discussion of organisational performance measures in Chapter 2.

More generally, this explanation of learning can help to explain apparently nonsensical behaviour. We may, for example, be unwittingly rewarding inappropriate behaviours because we fail to recognise what others may regard as a reward. If a child behaves badly to obtain attention, punishment (because it is at least better than no attention at all) may actually encourage the child to repeat the bad behaviour. If we punish an uncollaborative employee by excluding him or her from future teamworking, we may simply be reinforcing behaviour that is not in the wider interests of the organisation.

Despite its influence in the workplace and elsewhere, however, there is one major problem with the Behaviourist approach to learning. It assumes that nothing of psychological importance lies between the stimulus and the response – that there is a direct and automatic link between the two. This assumption helped theorists to explain, predict and control a person's behaviour without having to concern themselves with examining the content of people's minds. This is too simplistic a view, and explains the many definitions of learning which assume that learning only happens when a change in behaviour results. In practice, the relationship may be highly complex. To take a simple workplace example: a productivity bonus scheme may stimulate people to work faster and harder. But if the scheme makes unreasonable demands, it may also demotivate people, so that short-term performance improvements are achieved at the expense of longer-term problems of morale, attendance, employee turnover, and so on.

The Cognitive Approach recognises that something does indeed go on inside people's brains, and that this 'something' can be examined, if only by inference. Behaviourist approaches cannot explain, for example, how the same situation could be perceived by one employee as rewarding and by another as punishing. We might, for example, consider the example of a senior manager who always walks around the shop floor and asks employees for their opinions. One member of staff likes the recognition that this gives him, and goes out of his way to provide suggestions. Another sees it as being 'pestered' and 'watched over', and avoids entering into conversation with the manager.

One of the most useful principles of this approach relates to the concept of *feedback*. In simple terms, knowledge of past behaviour provides more insight into our actions and can influence future behaviour. Much use has been made of feedback within organisations, particularly under the guise of performance management. It is seldom well managed, however. Feedback must be provided as soon as possible after an event if it is to be effective. If the time between behaviour and feedback is too long – for example, if the only time an employee's performance is discussed is once a year as part of an annual appraisal process – then the whole learning process is rendered ineffective.

A study by Meyer (1985) showed that on average appraisees received at least 13 criticisms in each interview. This resulted in the appraisees' becoming defensive and negative towards the whole process. Other studies have revealed that when there is recognition of good performance together with some negative feedback, the process is more likely to be regarded by the appraisees as very useful in helping learning and performance change.

Models of learning

How, then, does learning take place? A number of commentators have attempted to develop systematic models of the processes that take place in learning. One of the most influential of these is that of Kolb and Rubin (1974), who describe learning as a four-stage cycle (see Figure 10).

Figure 10

THE LEARNING CYCLE

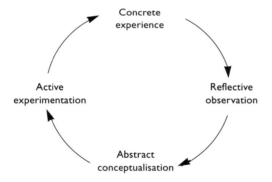

Concrete experience is the stage in which there is learning from feeling, from specific experiences, or from relating to people and being sensitive to their feelings.

Reflective Observation is the stage in the cycle in which people learn from 'thinking back' on what happened, or by observing other people in a situation. It involves careful observation, looking for the meaning of events.

Abstract Conceptualisation involves learning by using logic, ideas and theories, rather than feelings, to understand problems or situations. It involves learning by thinking and by systematic planning.

Active Experimentation involves learning by doing, experimenting with influencing or changing situations. It involves taking notes and influencing people and events through action.

Kolb and Rubin suggest that learning only takes place if people go through all of the stages of the learning cycle. For example, a graduate applies for a number of jobs through the annual milk-round and gets through to the interview stage on a number of occasions. He goes along to the first interview – and it is a disaster. He may leave it there and go away feeling uncomfortable, nothing learned from the situation except that it was an uncomfortable experience. If, however, he progresses a stage further on the learning cycle, he may think back on the situation and reflect on what happened. He was asked questions he could not answer; there was an 'awkward' feeling from the moment he was invited into the interview room; the interviewer appeared to 'talk down' to him throughout the interview. Again he could leave it there, or he could analyse the situation further, perhaps read a book on interviewing skills. He may then realise that he might have been better received had he not been wearing jeans and training shoes, if he had prepared for the kinds of questions he was likely to be asked, if he had answered his questions with more than a 'Yes' or 'No'. In itself, though, this discovery is still not enough. He needs to put his new knowledge into practice in the next interview he attends and not simply repeat the same mistakes. He will again go through the interview process, armed with this new information, and try out the new ways of preparing for the interview, dressing, and answering questions. The process then starts all over again.

It is clear that, at each stage, some learning has taken place. This again challenges the view that learning leads to changes in behaviour. In practice, not all learning experiences start and end with action. Often the process is continuous. A person can learn by starting at any point on the learning cycle. For example, students of management may, as yet, have had no experience of working in an organisation, let alone of managing a group of staff. When these students finally go out into the world of work and achieve their first managerial positions, they have the opportunity to put this learning into practice, provided they can remember the theories and provided that the learning event itself – the characteristics of the individual and the environment – allows for a transfer of learning to take place. In this case the students have begun with 'abstract conceptualisation' and proceeded round the learning cycle from there.

Kolb and Rubin note that very often people become 'stuck' in their preferred, or previously most successful, mode of learning and are seldom able to work their way easily around all parts of the learning cycle. Having identified preferred learning styles by means of an instrument called the 'Learning Styles Inventory', they describe the characteristics of four main kinds of learners who tend to have preferences for certain parts of the learning cycle:

☐ The *accommodator*, who learns mainly from combining the learning steps of concrete experience and active experimentation. People with this learning style have the ability to learn primarily from 'hands-on' experience, enjoy new experiences, may act on 'gut' feeling rather than on logical analysis, and prefer action careers such as sales and marketing.

☐ The *diverger*, who combines the learning steps of concrete experience and reflective observation. People with this learning style are best at viewing practical situations from a number of different points of view, and may tend to observe situations rather than take action. Because they tend to be imaginative and sensitive to the feelings of others, they may prefer to work in entertainment, caring or other service careers, such as nursing, the police or social work.

☐ The *converger*, who combines the learning steps of abstract conceptualisation and active experimentation. People with this learning style are good at finding ways to implement ideas and theories. They are able to solve problems and make decisions based on finding the best solution to questions or problems. They prefer working in technological areas, such as computing, engineering or medicine, in which finding the best solution is important.

☐ The *assimilator*, who combines the learning steps of abstract conceptualisation and reflective observation. People with this learning style enjoy working with abstract ideas and concepts, and concern themselves more with theories than practical situations. They enjoy working in areas such as teaching and research.

Another team of commentators, Honey and Mumford (1982), have taken more of a process approach to the learning cycle. They have simplified and refined Kolb's categories of learners into *activists* (who prefer to learn by doing), *reflectors* (who prefer to learn by observation), *theorists* (who prefer to learn by reading books and learning theories), and *pragmatists* (who learn by planning and by applying theories to practice). The instrument they use to assess preferred learning styles is called the 'LSQ' – The Learning Styles Questionnaire.

Their work has focused on developing the learning ability of managers by making them aware of their own preferred learning style and preferred learning activities. They have also highlighted the implications of learning style preferences in different organisational contexts. For example, many organisations that place a high value on action tend unwittingly to encourage 'firefighting', because employees and managers spend much of their time dealing with short-term problems, moving continually between planning and doing, without ever having the time to reflect and reach conclusions. On the other hand, students straight out of university may spend a lot of time reflecting and theorising without ever getting around to planning and action.

Clearly, managers should not be encouraged to focus solely on their preferred, or most successful, mode. Instead they should be encouraged to 'learn how to learn' by progressing right round the learning cycle, starting with their most effective learning mode and moving to their least effective style. Honey and Mumford note that a lot of designed learning events and methods are at odds with the preferences of the learner, and most commonly reflect the preferred style of the trainer, facilitator or teacher. For example, a theorist would not learn much from a role-play exercise, just as an activist would dislike sitting through a two-hour lecture.

Mumford notes that learning to learn brings benefits not only for the individual, but also for the organisation, notably

☐   an increase in the capacity of individuals to learn
☐   a reduction in the frustration of being exposed to inefficient

learning processes

☐ an increase in motivation to learn

☐ a recognition that unwillingness to learn from one particular activity is not generalisable as an unwillingness to learn from anything

☐ development of learning opportunities well beyond formally created situations

☐ a multiplier effect for the manager in his or her developmental relationship with his or her subordinates

☐ the reduction of dependence on a tutor

☐ the provision of processes which carry through beyond formal programmes into on-the-job learning

☐ the better identification of the role of learning in effective managerial behaviour, for example, in problem solving or teamwork

☐ the development of more effective behaviour in relation to the crucial subject of change.

Learning to learn has been frequently described as a 'meta-competence' and as being essential to an individual's and an organisation's ability to change and to survive in an increasingly turbulent environment. Increasingly, organisations are perceiving learning as a critical element of competitive advantage, and it has been said that an organisation's ability to compete is only as good as its members' ability to learn.

Honey and Mumford have conducted research into preferred learning styles across various disciplines and across different countries. For example, they found that sales managers tended to be more action-oriented activist-pragmatists, whereas police sergeants tend to be more reflector-theorists. Interestingly, they found that finance managers tended to be theorists. Similarly, research undertaken by Dalziel and Anderson (1994) into the learning styles of undergraduate students revealed that students from different disciplines had significantly different learning styles. For example, engineering students tended to be predominantly activists, whereas occupational therapists tended to be predominantly reflectors.

We can conclude that individuals learn in different ways depending upon the learning mode they find most comfortable and to which they are most accustomed. We need to consider carefully, therefore, where in the learning cycle learning (and specifically training) should start. Traditional training courses usually start with the input of knowledge, including perhaps some reflection on past experience and maybe a video to observe, followed by some planning of how this may be applied back at work. It is often left to chance whether the new learning is applied in a real-life work situation, and there is, not surprisingly, a frequent problem of poor transfer of learning from such courses. This can be resolved in part by, for example, the use of learning contracts and follow-on courses to report on implementation issues, followed by reflection, the drawing of conclusions, and planning for next time. This encourages trainees to go continually right around the learning cycle, using areas with which they are usually less comfortable.

Other training approaches – such as structured on-the-job coaching – start with action, followed by reflection on this experience, the drawing of conclusions, planning for next time, and efforts to apply the required new behaviours. Again the process is likely to be most effective if the participant is taken systematically around the learning cycle. Evidence suggests that if employees learn to learn using modes with which they are less comfortable, they can at least double their learning capability.

The US commentator Nedd Hermann has proposed a further model, *brain dominance*, which also suggests a holistic approach to learning and development. Hermann proposes that the brain is composed not only of two hemispheres but of four quadrants, each with its own areas of specialisation. He divides the brain into left/right hemispheres and into cerebral/limbic functioning. Cerebral-left thinking preferences (quadrant A) are characterised as logical, analytical, fact-based and quantitative. People with this quadrant A dominance learn best by applying analysis and logic to situations, thinking through ideas and forming theories. They respond best to lectures, use of textbooks, and technical case discussions.

Limbic-left thinking (quadrant B) is sequential, organised, detailed and planned. People with this quadrant dominant learn best by acquiring skills through practice, evaluating and testing theories. They respond best to highly structured learning situations, such as programmed learning, lectures and thorough planning.

Limbic-right thinking preferences (quadrant C) are characterised as interpersonal, feeling-based, kinaesthetic, and emotional. People with this quadrant dominant learn by emotional involvement, listening and sharing ideas. They respond best to experiential opportunities and group interactions.

Cerebral-right thinking (quadrant D) is holistic, intuitive, integrating and synthesising. People with this quadrant dominant learn best by exploring hidden possibilities, taking initiatives and synthesising ideas. They respond best to situations that involve spontaneity, experimentation, visual displays and anything that allows them to become involved.

Hermann adds that even when one or two quadrants are dominant within an individual, we are all a coalition of the quadrants/modes within the Whole Brain Model. The most effective learning, therefore, is likely to take place when individuals progress through a range of learning styles and experiences.

Dennis Martin of the Hermann Institute has suggested that a learning programme designed by a predominantly left-brained individual will be highly structured, lacking in creativity, and may not appeal to people with a predominant right-brain dominance. In the same way a programme designed by a right-brain trainer can be seen as unstructured and sloppy by a left-brained individual. Martin suggests that programmes should be 'whole-brained' and involve the use not only of both hemispheres but of all four quadrants – ie it should be logical, structured, creative, and involve emotion and feeling. In this way the programme in addition to incorporating something that will appeal to everyone will also facilitate the 'stretching' of individuals and encourage them to use different learning modes as appropriate.

Overall, therefore, there seems to be abundant evidence that different learning preferences exist, even if there are debates about the extent to which these preferences are innate or acquired. What, then, are the implications of such preferences for learning within organisations? Traditional training courses and academic courses in which there is a high level of input from the trainer clearly satisfy only those individuals with a particular learning preference. Methods based in learning from practical experience, such as action learning, need to be built into an organisation's overall learning processes. But this can be difficult to organise and sustain. So how should we structure our approaches to learning in organisations?

Different approaches to learning

Honey and Mumford, in their *Manual of Learning Opportunities* (1989), identify four different approaches to learning:

- ☐ *The Intuitive Approach* – People who believe they learn by this approach assume that learning happens as a result of experience. They believe learning is a natural process which 'just happens' by virtue of being in a particular situation.

- ☐ *The Incidental Approach* – People who use this approach to learning again learn by chance, but 'mull over' what happened after an event, sometimes discussing it with other people and noting down anything that may be worth considering in the future. They may believe that you cannot learn from routine situations, only from mistakes.

- ☐ *The Retrospective Approach* – People who use this approach, like the incidental approach, learn from looking back on an event after it has happened – yet they try to reach conclusions about the event to help them learn for the future. They learn from routine and from successful situations as well as from mistakes.

- ☐ *The Prospective Approach* – As well as looking back over an event after it has happened, people who learn from this approach go into a situation meaning to learn something from it. This makes them more effective at learning than people who use predominantly the other three approaches. Perhaps predictably, this approach appears to be used least often.

We might conclude, therefore, that a performance management system that encourages staff to learn using the prospective approach – that is, where employees are encouraged to plan what they want to learn in advance of a learning opportunity – is vastly superior to those that rely purely on reflection. This reinforces the view that, for example, appraisal processes which emphasise the developmental approach have a greater impact on learning than those which simply reflect on past experience for the purposes of establishing pay. In the same way, learning situations which encourage the identification of learning opportunities and the establishment of learning objectives (such as the use of learning contracts, learning logs and action learning) also prove to be more effective in the long term.

Blocks to learning and development

Hunter (1995) argued that employees have to be 'willing, able and allowed' to learn. Only then does learning really take place, and only then is this new learning put into practice. Employees must *want* to learn something new – that is, there must be some kind of perceived benefit in it for them, such as promotion, recognition, transfer to another job, or simply a desire to perform better in their existing jobs. They must be *able* to learn, not only in the physical and mental sense, but also in the provision of opportunities. Most importantly – and most often ignored – they have to be *allowed* to learn – that is, the organisation must not only encourage learning and risk-taking but they must remove common blocks to learning, such as aspects of the culture, managerial attitudes and beliefs, or systems and procedures that commonly prevent learning.

Some of these more common blocks to learning relate to

- desire for action at any cost
- lack of opportunities to put new learning into practice, because 'it has always been done this way'
- denying that there is a problem and therefore asserting that there is no need for any learning
- an unsupportive learning environment
- training as the only form of learning considered
- managers' not accepting responsibility for their staffs' learning
- determination not to try anything new for fear of failing
- fear of having to take on new work as a regular part of the job

- decisions that cannot be made on simple issues without approval's being sought first
- conformity's being perceived as essential
- an absence or low level of feedback regarding performance
- poor self-image and low confidence levels
- inappropriate behaviours' being rewarded by the organisation.

A classic quotation reported by Bob Garratt in *The Learning Organisation*, from a senior manager in the telecommunications industry, says much about attitudes to learning – 'I do not pay my managers to think. If they are going to think then they can do it in their own time on a Sunday.'

Some 'new' managerial initiatives can also act as major blocks to learning if they are applied inappropriately or over-rigorously. For example, the use of inappropriate and inflexible quality procedures to achieve British quality standards (such as BS5750) may stifle creativity or individual decision-making. Similarly, the overuse of the competence model of behaviour – particularly where success is measured by 'being competent' or 'not being competent' within a particular job role – may restrict further development. If the individual is assessed as 'being competent', there is no perceived need for further learning.

On the other hand, continuous development can be attained by enabling individuals to work their way around the learning cycle. These individuals nonetheless need to be motivated to learn and encouraged to use a range of learning styles. In addition, and perhaps most importantly, they require the removal of any organisational blocks and barriers to learning.

The learning organisation

If we really succeed in achieving all of the above objectives, it is no longer appropriate to think of learning purely in terms of the individual. Through the learning ability of the organisation as a whole – that is, through collective learning processes – we are able to achieve continuous improvement in *corporate* performance. This concept is sometimes referred to as the 'Learning Organisation'.

Pedler, Burgoyne and Boydell provided one of the earliest

definitions of the learning organisation as 'an organisation which facilitates the learning of all its members and continually transforms itself'. A more recent definition by Peter Senge expands this view slightly and defines learning organisations as 'organisations where people continually expand their capacity to create the results they truly desire, where new and expansive patterns of thinking are nurtured, where collective aspiration is set free, and where people are continually learning how to learn together.'

A learning organisation is clearly more than the sum of all the learning that takes place within the organisation. It is about creating a future for the organisation by having all members of the learning organisation move around the learning cycle. Hedberg, for example, has argued that 'Although organisational learning occurs through individuals, it would be a mistake to conclude that organisational learning is nothing but the cumulative result of their members' learning. Organisations do not have brains, but they have cognitive systems and memories ... organisations' memories preserve certain behaviours, mental maps, norms and values over time.' In this context, change is no longer about establishing an end-point in the change process and achieving it by a number of logical sequential steps. It is rather about continually changing and adapting, without always being clear about where you are going but always being fully responsive to changes in the external environment.

This view of shared learning leading to a shared understanding helps to explain how an organisational culture can develop over time and at the same time be dependent on the organisation's history. This involves, in effect, a movement from the individual conscious to the collective unconscious. For example, many organisations – particularly those that are more bureaucratic – rely on tight systems and procedures to 'keep discipline' and retain control over their subordinates. As a result, most behaviour within the organisation conforms to this defined standard, including the provision of information about internal processes and external environmental forces. Managers tend to be told what they want to hear, in order to reinforce the views they already hold and confirm that they were 'right all along'. There is virtually nothing in the way of experimentation or the testing of ideas. When a problem arises, it is dealt with through the establishment of a 'blame' culture, followed by an accompanying witch-hunt.

The learning organisation, as we have described it, is the polar opposite of this traditional bureaucracy. Some have argued that a true learning organisation can never exist and remains only a theoretical concept. In the pure sense, this may be true. In most organisations, however, it is possible to make useful progress towards this ideal. Any move in this direction helps to ensure the survival of the organisation in times when change is so rapid and unpredictable and the environment so turbulent.

Becoming a learning organisation

Argyris and Schon describe a familiar process of organisational learning that limits the organisation's ability to change. They call this process 'single loop learning'. They make the analogy between single loop learning and a thermostat which, if it is set at 70°C, switches the heating mechanism on and off to ensure that a constant temperature is retained. They note that most organisations, when faced with a problem, really only ever go around the single loop, and respond to problems by means of carrying out more or less of a particular behavioural response. For example, an economic development organisation may find that employers are making little use of one of its employment initiatives to encourage employees to recruit from the unemployed population. The organisation responds simply by increasing advertising to ensure that enough people have heard about the scheme. Single loop learning is characterised by 'stop-go' behaviour, applying 'more of' or 'less of' the same treatment.

In practice, the reason for the poor uptake of the programme may be more deep-rooted, requiring greater analysis and a different way of thinking. For example, it may be appropriate to consider whether the scheme is actually offering a service that is required or is beneficial to employers. This questioning approach provides greater insight into the situation and allows for greater learning to take place. Such an approach of questioning and challenging is called double loop learning. To extend the metaphor used by Argyris and Schon, it would require the thermostat to explain why it was set at 70°C in the first place! How often in meetings, when someone challenges the underlying assumptions, are they told that these issues are 'not relevant' to the discussion? After this response, the meeting quickly reverts to single loop learning.

Swieringa and Wierdsma add a third loop, producing triple loop learning. This refers to changes in the communally-shared principles on which the system is based. We might, for example, ask fundamental questions – what kind of organisation do we wish to be? What contribution do we want to make? What values do we consider important? The economic development organisation, at this level of learning, may decide that it should not attempt to deal with problems of unemployment but should set itself other objectives.

In short, the learning organisation is one that enables effective learning among all its members, and that applies this learning to question, develop and improve its overall role and activities. In this context, performance management at both the individual and the organisational level is a process of continuous improvement. We learn from our experiences, and we use this learning, in a structured and systematic manner, to take us forward. As we move towards the twenty-first century, and as the pace of organisational and environmental change becomes ever faster, effective learning becomes a more and more critical tool for managing and improving performance. Reg Revans – one of the pioneers of Action Learning – noted that if an organisation is to survive, its rate of learning must be equal to or greater than the rate of change in its environment. Peter Honey makes the same point more succinctly, asserting that 'Change is learning, learning is change. You can't have one without the other.'

8

PERFORMANCE-RELATED PAY

Ashley Richardson

In the preceding chapters we have examined the range of tools and techniques that contribute to effective performance management – objective-setting, performance measurement, appraisal, learning, and development. In this chapter we consider the final piece of the performance management jigsaw. For many organisations, performance management is unlikely to be effective unless, in some way, it is explicitly linked to the way people are paid. Although there may be continuing debate about the relationship between pay and motivation, an increasing number of organisations appear to have accepted in practice that employees should receive an element of their pay or their pay rise on the basis of 'performance'. For commission-only staff, such as many salesmen, the whole of their pay is performance-related. For the majority, however, the performance-related element is much smaller – and sometimes relatively insignificant. Similarly, some pay rises are totally linked to increases in performance. Others combine a general increase with an additional performance-related element.

When performance pay was first introduced, schemes tended to focus on purely individual results or outputs, and paid no regard to the method of achieving those outputs. Performance pay of this kind tended to encourage certain types of behaviour which were not always those actually sought by the employer. For example, they typically took no account of such variables as costs, quality, customer satisfaction, team-working, or personal development. For example, a salesman might deliver his targets by reducing prices to an unacceptable level, or by 'over-selling' the benefits of a particular product so that customers later become dissatisfied.

Because of such problems there has now been a trend away from individual schemes to those which reward overall organisational performance by measuring individual/group inputs or behaviours as well as outputs. Moreover, many performance-related pay schemes are now designed not only to encourage improvement in corporate performance, but also to encourage the type of cultures (or culture change) required by the overall business goal and style of management. We consider some of these options in more detail below.

Some have also argued that, in a global economy where labour productivity is an increasingly critical factor, the days of the universal annual pay rise have gone. Instead, any changes in pay should not only be directly linked to the fortunes of the organisation as a whole, but should also be distributed to employees in ways that reflect behaviours which contribute to success.

Whatever the approach adopted, however, the objectives of performance-related pay remain the same:

☐ to focus reward on contribution
☐ to improve motivation and commitment
☐ to encourage acceptance and participation in changing procedures and processes.

Above all, the purpose of performance-related pay must be to reinforce the performance goals and priorities determined by the organisation. If the performance pay system is aligned with the organisation's performance needs, pay can become, in effect, the fuel that drives the overall performance management process. However, if – as so often happens – the performance pay system is not aligned to wider performance needs, it can serve only to undermine whatever performance management activities are taking place elsewhere.

Making performance-related pay work

In a survey published by the Industrial Society in 1994, 48 per cent of contributors reported that their pay was directly linked to the results of a performance appraisal. In turn, the performance appraisal process focused on a number of performance measures, including the achievement of objectives (reported by 40 per cent of respondents), standards of performance (35 per cent) and key result areas (15 per cent), 51 per cent of the respondents had revisited their performance management system within the precious two years, and the allocation of performance-related pay increases had been one of the major areas of change over the same two years.

As these figures suggest, pay can be linked to performance in a variety of ways. The most important factor, however, is to ensure a link between performance-related pay and the behaviour and effort required for success. This can be achieved in various ways, which we will discuss later, but – as we have emphasised repeatedly in this book – all need to be part of an overall strategy for the business as a whole. The link is likely to be most successful when it is used to reinforce cultural change initiatives and to establish a firm and clearly understood relationship between pay and performance. In particular, the link needs to be focused and communicated on the basis of *shared* improvements in performance. It is no coincidence that many of the more robust and influential performance pay schemes are developed through joint participation by both management and employees – including, in many cases, the involvement of trade unions. If employees understand and accept the basis on which performance is being evaluated, half the battle is won.

At the same time, we need to recognise that performance pay is not a panacea that automatically cures all an organisation's performance problems. There is limited evidence to support the view that performance pay has an inherently positive effect on many individuals, and there is limited evidence that performance pay is a genuine motivator. Indeed, performance pay can be accused of having several disadvantages, particularly if the system is unfairly or inconsistently applied. For example, individual performance payments can often be divisive, especially if the overall approach to performance management and appraisal is poorly designed and open to manipulation. Moreover, individualised performance pay, unless it is very carefully designed and applied, almost inevitably intensifies competition between employees and undermines teamworking. This may be fine if it suits the needs of the organisation (for example, if employees are engaged largely in solo activities with little need for collaboration), but can be disastrous if teamworking is a priority.

When it is properly designed and managed, however, performance pay can bring significant benefits to the organisation – and not least of these is to help focus effort on the real challenges facing an organisation, while allowing the management of the pay bill to reflect the fortunes of the company as a whole.

Approaches to performance-related pay

Approaches and designs of performance-related pay schemes fall into three distinct categories – those that reward the performance of

□ individuals

□ teams or groups

□ organisations as a whole.

In many cases, organisation or business strategy may require the use of all three categories at different times as the strategy develops. The most common trend is to determine the level of bonus payment on the basis of organisational performance, but then to distribute the payment of the bonus on the basis of organisation goals or needs. For example, let us say that, due to the overall performance of the business, the organisation is able to increase the pay bill by 6 per cent in the following year. This could be distributed as

□ 1.5 per cent to *all* employees (or alternatively variable amounts according to grade) as a general company bonus

□ 2 per cent to the groups or teams that achieved or exceeded their targets or provided other major performance improvements

□ 2.5 per cent to individuals through the performance appraisal system according to individual delivery of targets, competence development or promotion.

In another year, not only might the overall budget change to reflect the organisational performance, but also these relative proportions could change to reflect the changing needs of the organisation in terms of, say, behaviours or performance requirements.

There are several ways of rewarding performance that can be applied, to a greater or lesser extent, depending on the contributions of employees and the environment in which they are operating. Each approach has its advantages and disadvantages which need to be clearly understood.

Piecework and measured work schemes

Piecework schemes are based purely on the output achieved by the individual (or, occasionally, by a team or group). A standard payment is made for each unit produced. The amount paid is based on costing considerations, and no regard is given to the actual length of time taken to produce the output. The equation is, quite simply: the more produced, the greater the pay. Some schemes have included graduated payments, and there is no doubt that if piecework is to be effective the process should be subject to rigorous quality standards and inspection procedures. Without these, employees may be encouraged to increase their output at the expense of quality. Some employers also guarantee a minimum income in order to ensure some loyalty from their employees and to compensate for factors such as operational downtime or the employer's failure to provide a constant flow of raw materials.

Piecework is most suitable to manufacturing industries in which highly repetitious production runs are carried out and where a high level of manual input is required. It is also most appropriate to those organisations (of any type) which believe that money is the main motivator of their workforce. It is important to ensure that output (and therefore payment) is not unduly constrained by factors outside the employees' control – so, for example, product change-over times must be short, and the onus is on the employer to provide a continuous flow of work and raw materials. Moreover, as we indicate above, high levels of supervision and inspection are needed if quality and safety standards are to be maintained.

Piecework is also suitable for organisations that manufacture 'craft'-type products of which quality standards are less regulated and where the safety and integrity of raw materials is not an issue. Piecework is also often applied to outworkers by this type of organisation. Piecework may also be appropriate for clerical and administrative staff by whom large amounts of repetitive transactions are processed either off or on site. For example, many financial services organisations are setting up central 'processing factories' so that various forms of routine administration and data processing can be handled as efficiently as possible. Piecework may well be appropriate to such operations, although they require the same kinds of controls as more traditional manufacturing operations.

The advantages of piecework are that

□ it is easy to predict the costs of production as long as quality standards are maintained
□ it is simple to operate and relatively difficult to misinterpret
□ it allows employees to directly link effort to performance and therefore determine how much they earn
□ it rewards high producers.

The disadvantages of piecework, however, are that

□ it requires high levels of supervision and inspection
□ it can cause problems with quality standards because only outputs are valued
□ it leads to a resistance to changes in working methods and to the introduction of new machinery
□ it can cause employee dissatisfaction if continuous work-flows and materials are not provided
□ it demands little loyalty from the employee, which leads to a lack of teamwork
□ it provides no incentive to identify and share improvements in working methods
□ it can be difficult to renegotiate targets and payment levels
□ it can reduce control over the levels of production or output.

Measured work schemes are similar to piecework but reward employees on the basis of the time taken to carry out a specified piece of work. Using method study (to identify the most efficient method of operation) and work measurement techniques, a standard time is calculated for carrying out the given task or sequence of activities. The employee is then rewarded for time saved in carrying out the activities. As with piecework, there are a number of variations on this basic theme. In some cases the employee is rewarded for any improvements above a basic level. In others, pay is reduced as the employee falls below the defined 'standard' level. In some cases reward may be directly proportional to the level of improvement achieved. In others, a differential scale may be applied so that the relative level of reward increases (or decreases) as further improvements are achieved.

The benefits and disadvantages of measured work schemes are (not surprisingly, in that it essentially applies the same principle in reverse) very similar to those of piecework. It can be an effective approach in production environments involving a high level of repetitive work, particularly if there has traditionally been significant variation in the levels of individual productivity. At the same time, it does require a high level of control, both over the overall process and over the quality of individual outputs.

Measured day work is a further variation on the basic theme of 'payment by results', designed to help overcome some of the unpredictability of piecework or measured work schemes. Under a measured day work scheme the employee is paid a fixed supplementary payment if he or she maintains an agreed level of production over a specified period. Again, the required level of production is set on the basis of work measurement techniques. It is also possible to determine several production levels, linked to increasingly high payments, so that the employee can progress through these as his or her productivity increases.

The attraction of measured day work is that it removes much of the uncertainty associated with piecework while still providing a direct link between pay and output. Its advantages and disadvantages are again similar to those of piecework, although arguably its relative predictability brings benefits both to the employer (who can predict production costs more accurately) and to the employee (who suffers less variation in pay levels). In practice, the evidence suggests that measured day work schemes, like other forms of payment by results, require careful design and monitoring.

Incremental or appraisal-based schemes

Traditional 'payment by results' schemes, such as those described above, are appropriate only where individual contribution to productivity can be easily and accurately measured – for example, on a production line or some form of 'craft'-based assembly process. If we wish to link pay to performance in situations in which productivity is less easily measured – such as administrative or managerial roles – we have to adopt more qualitative ways of assessing and rewarding individual contribution. In most cases, as was discussed in Chapter 6, this is through some form of qualitative performance appraisal or rating.

Most commonly, the payment or salary range for the job is determined through some form of job evaluation, and the performance appraisal process is used to determine how quickly the individual progresses through this range. There are numerous variations on this basic theme. Perhaps the most familiar approach – widely used particularly in the public sector – is the 'incremental scheme' whereby employees progress through a series of predetermined steps to the top of the salary scale. In its simplest form the increment is paid automatically on an annual basis so long as the individual is judged to have performed satisfactorily. More sophisticated approaches allow the appraising manager to withhold all or part of the increment for below-average performance or to pay additional increments for above-average performance.

Although an increasing number of organisations have moved away from the traditional fixed-increment approach, it may be an effective way of rewarding performance in situations in which individual performance can be expected to improve over time, but in which it is difficult to assess individual contribution with any precision. It is easily understood and – particularly if there is at least some scope to recognise above- and below-average performance – is likely to be perceived as broadly equitable. If we tend to perceive pay essentially as a means of rewarding past and current contribution, rather than as a tool to motivate future performance, then the incremental approach may be satisfactory. Moreover, if the organisation is dependent on collective or team contributions, an incremental approach may be perceived as a fair way of recognising individual experience without promoting an overly individual-istic ethic.

The weakness of the incremental approach, however, is that it does not permit significant discrimination between, say, poor, average, and excellent performers. Indeed, if the payment of the increment is largely automatic, it may actually be perceived as *inequitable*, because poor performers are rewarded on the same basis as their more capable colleagues. For this reason, an increasing number of organisations, in order to promote a greater emphasis on individual performance, have introduced *merit-based* schemes. Under such a scheme, although the overall salary range is again determined by job evaluation, pay increases are variable and directly linked to individual performance ratings.

Again there are numerous variations on this theme. In some cases there is a fixed formula linking rating to reward. In others, there is no fixed formula, and local managers may be allowed to exercise discretion in the distribution of pay increases within a fixed overall budget.

Although merit schemes have become increasingly popular in recent years, their effectiveness has also often been ques-tioned. Their strength is that they allow the organisation to target its rewards as precisely as possible on those who are seen as the most effective performers. Their weakness is that they are dependent on the application of a highly effective perfor-mance measurement and appraisal process. If the appraisal process is perceived as ineffective, biased or inaccurate, the merit scheme rapidly loses credibility and is likely to under-mine, rather than enhance, individual and organisational performance. Even if the appraisal process is perceived as effec-tive, the merit pay scheme may have undesired side-effects. It may, for example, undermine team goals or performance – although it may be possible to overcome this in part by includ-ing 'contribution to team performance' as one of the performance criteria.

Group- or organisation-wide schemes

The above approaches are all, in their various ways, designed to recognise and reward individual performance. Many organ-isations have in recent years moved towards such schemes because they feel that traditionally there has been too little emphasis on individual contribution. It is also true, however, that some organisations have sought to introduce schemes which perhaps more accurately reflect the *interdependency* of collective contribution. In other words, rather than rewarding individual performance, they reward collective performance – whether of the work-group, of the department, or of the company as a whole.

At the simplest level, this includes pay linked to corporate performance or profit. Profit-related pay, in its various forms, may be a useful tool, both to help challenge traditional expectations of pay increases not linked to organisational performance, and to encourage greater employee awareness of profitability as an issue. Because the individual employee's contribution to overall profitability is likely to be fairly remote, however, it is unlikely to be a direct motivator to individual performance.

More pertinent methods may include bonuses or pay increases linked to team or departmental performance (or, in more complex schemes, to performance against some combination of team and individual performance objectives). A more sophisticated variation may be some form of *gainsharing*, by which employees (as well as the organisation) share in a bonus pool created by improvements in added value created by the employees. This last approach, if carefully constructed, may be a particularly powerful tool for encouraging collective problem-solving and performance improvement.

Skill- or competency-based pay

The above schemes, whether individual or collective, are all designed to recognise and reward *outputs*. It is also possible, however, for performance pay schemes to focus on inputs – that is, the capabilities or qualities that the individual brings to the job. The logic here is that if the individual brings the right qualities to his or her work, improved performance results. Some organisations, for example, have introduced skill-based pay schemes under which employees receive pay increases for the acquisition of particular skills. Such schemes are most common in an organisation that is trying to achieve some particular shift in its overall skill-set (for example, where the organisation wishes to increase employee flexibility through multi-skilling). Skill-based schemes tend to be temporary because the scheme becomes irrelevant once the majority of staff have achieved the required skill levels.

Although skill-based schemes can be a powerful tool for achieving a specific organisation development objective, their weakness is that they reward employees simply for the acquisition of the skill, whether or not it is applied. Competency-based schemes, however, take this a stage further by linking reward to the *demonstration of required behaviours* (which may involve particular styles, values or approaches as well as skills). Under such schemes the individual is rewarded not simply for acquiring a particular skill but for demonstrating, satisfactorily and consistently, that he or she behaves in a particular way. The organisation might, for example, define required competencies in areas such as people management, teamworking or leadership. An increasing number of organisations are introducing competency-based schemes – not least because this approach is seen as providing a relatively tangible way of dealing with the cultural and stylistic aspects of performance.

Selecting a performance pay scheme
As this brief summary suggests, there is no 'right' approach to performance-related pay. Although some have seen individualised merit pay (for example) as a universal panacea, there is a growing body of evidence to suggest that, at best, it can be helpful only in certain organisational circumstances, and that – if it is applied carelessly or inappropriately – it may have a damaging effect on performance.

In practice, performance pay can rarely be applied in isolation. It needs to be seen as part of the overall performance management process – a tool that can be used to reinforce (or, just as easily, to undermine) the other elements we describe in this book. If are to apply performance pay effectively, therefore, we need to consider it in this strategic context. We need to consider, for instance,

□ the overall performance objectives of the organisation
□ the specific performance objectives of particular work-

groups or departments

□ the ways in which these objectives might develop (for example, our short-term objectives may be different from our long-term needs)

□ the history and culture of the organisation.

The last point is particularly important, because the organisation's culture may militate against our preferred approach to pay. If the organisation has traditionally operated a fixed-increment scheme, we may be asking too much if we shift overnight to a fully individualised merit scheme, even if it is justified by our organisational needs and objectives. The resulting culture shock may demotivate employees rather than improve performance. In this context we may be better off applying some interim approach, the more radical scheme being a longer-term objective.

In essence, though, our chosen approach needs to reflect our organisational objectives. If we perceive, say, innovation or teamworking as key performance requirements for the organisation, we need to establish a payment scheme that will reinforce (or, at least, not undermine) these qualities. On the other hand, if our prime objective is to sustain or improve productivity, perhaps some simpler payment-by-results scheme is appropriate. Whichever scheme we choose, though, we need to recognise that pay, by itself, cannot improve performance. It may (perhaps) motivate employees. It may encourage them to work towards certain goals. It may help to change expectations or culture. But if employees are really to improve their performance, pay needs to be just one element in the overall package of guidance, encouragement and support that we have defined as performance management.

It may be helpful here to consider a real-life case study of how one organisation applied performance pay as a tool to underpin wider organisational performance objectives.

Case study: Pearl Assurance

Pearl Assurance is a major financial institution offering a full range of pensions and insurances to its 2.5 million policyholders. It is now owned by AMP, an Australian insurance company. It works out of 150 offices in Britain and employs around 10,000 people, of which 4,500 work in sales, 5,500 are administrative staff, and the remaining 3,000 work in the Head Office in Peterborough. Its staff are represented by the MSF.

Gareth Trevor joined Pearl in 1992, from ICL, as general manager, human resources. Part of his brief was to review and introduce a revised performance management and performance-related payment structure. When he arrived he was faced with 14 appraisal schemes and a situation in which line managers designed their own methods, amid a general belief that it was possible to pay for performance without measuring it.

There was a need to

☐ change behaviour and to increase performance considerably,
☐ focus on increased customer satisfaction
☐ increase the levels of skill competence and qualifications within the company.

Gareth believes that performance-related pay is only a small part of the performance management process which rewards people for what they have done. On its own, performance-related pay does not improve performance and should be seen as a reward, not an incentive. To be successful, any scheme needs to start with a clear picture of

☐ what is wanted
☐ what people have to do in order to achieve what is wanted
☐ how the process will be reviewed.

The performance management system that exists today has been introduced in stages, the last people entering the system in January 1995. It is a system that is not clearly linked with performance because very few staff – between 5 and 10 per cent – think of themselves as high performers. Instead it rewards people according to their market worth and the level of commitment shown.

The performance management process now in place is indivisibly linked to business performance as a whole. The Organisation Management Review (OMR) is a series of formal reviews which take place at company and departmental level.

This activity is carried out by the Pearl management team at least twice a year, and by functional managers about two to three times a year. The aim of the OMR is to plan for the succession and development of employees.

The Review looks at the current organisation structure and assesses the extent to which it is appropriate to current and predicted requirements. Every individual is then reviewed and gaps identified in knowledge, skills and experience. This then produces a plan of the overall training and development needs both for individuals and for training and personnel managers.

During the last four years, restructuring has led to a leaner, flatter structure comprising only eight grades. This has resulted in turn in fewer promotional opportunities but increased scope for greater job rotation and the development of wider skills and competencies through cross-functional transfers and projects.

Each individual has a performance management folder which moves around the company with him or her, going wherever the individual is assigned to a project for more than three months. Each manager is required to hold a formal review of the individual's performance at most every six months and to continuously coach and review, thus ensuring any necessary corrective action is swiftly taken.

The individual roles are defined in a Career Atlas, which analyses the various functions and key roles within each function. Each of these roles is then defined in terms of technical skills and behavioural competencies required. These competencies fall into five clusters:

- *leading people*
  individual leadership
  meeting leadership
  visionary leadership
  strategic leadership
- *managing people*
  delegation
  developing organisational talent
  maximising performance
  motivational fit
  empowerment

☐ *communicating*
  impact
  meeting membership
  negotiation
  oral communication
  oral presentation
  written communication
  sales ability/persuasiveness
  teamwork/co-operation
  collaboration

☐ *Personal*
  ability to learn
  adaptability
  initiative
  tolerance of stress
  tenacity
  resilience
  physical health/ability
  integrity
  energy
  innovation

☐ *managing work*
  analysis (problem identification)
  customer service orientation
  follow-up
  information monitoring
  judgement (problem-solution)
  planning and organising
  technical/professional knowledge
  work standards
  safety awareness
  keyboard skills
  attention to detail
  business acumen
  external perspective.

This framework is used for the purposes of recruitment, promotion, career development, and individual and organisational development.

Each individual is appraised annually against the competency framework, and personal performance improvements and development needs are identified. They are judged thus not only against what they are expected to do and achieve but also against how they do it, through the development of competencies and skills that increase the flexibility and value of the employee to the company. Each individual is then graded on a scale of one to five, and a training and development plan is targeted for the next year. The individual development plan is then recorded in personal development folder.

The individual ratings are:

1   Exceptional
2   Very good
3   Good
4   Needs improvement
5   Not acceptable
N   New to the job

Pay guidelines are issued annually, and prior to any review the company determines the overall amount it wishes to spend on increases. Senior managers are then told how much is available in financial and percentage terms for distribution to staff in their function. The functional managers then determine how much is available for each department (this may vary according to the performance of each department).

The actual pay rise for the individual is dependent on two factors: performance, and the position of the individual in the scale. Basically, two people in the same grade who gain the same performance rating should be paid roughly the same and get the same pay rise.

The salary scales themselves are reviewed each year against comprehensive market data but do not change automatically against rises in the cost of living. Most grades have a spread from 70 to 130 per cent of the mid-point. Progression through the grades depends on the performance rating given in the appraisal and the amount of money allowed in the pay guidelines.

For those identified as having a performance rating of 3 and worse, the maximum salary is set at 115 per cent of the mid-point. Those rated as having performed either exceptionally or very well can progress up to 130 per cent of the mid-point.

Exceptionally, market pressures on certain groups of specialist staff can lead to premium rates being paid outside the evaluated band, but generally this system means that staff paid above 115 per cent of the mid-point and graded at 3 or worse do not receive a pay rise. This should, in times of inflation and higher pay rises, reduce anomalies to a minimum. However, in times of low inflation, such anomalies take longer to remove. This has proved particularly problematic at Pearl due to their past policy of paying premium rates, and still causes some disgruntlement among some highly paid but lower-performing staff who have not received any pay rise for a number of years.

Additionally, line management have available a small budget of around 0.75 per cent which they can use as a discretionary bonus for outstanding individual performance. It is interesting to note that this fund is consistently underspent.

In a fast-changing and highly competitive financial services market, customers expect and demand speedy and highly efficient service levels. Customer service was identified as one the key determinants of whether a customer comes back or becomes a customer at all. Customers expect the person on the other end of the telephone not only to be the expert in any of the 20 different product ranges that are sold, but also be able to recall instantly what any of your 1,500 colleagues said last month or last year.

Because each day the 20,000 inquiries that come into Head Office are handled by different departments, it was decided that the form of behaviour most needed among the staff who handle these calls was teamworking. To encourage this, it was decided to introduce team-based pay.

In an IMS study of 200 blue-chip companies surveyed, 40 per cent have introduced formal teamworking initiatives, but fewer than 4 per cent have introduced a pay policy to support them. Many have tried and failed. One of the main difficulties is the definition of what a team is.

The criteria applied at Pearl are:

☐ all the members are engaged in achieving a common output
☐ all the jobs are interdependent
☐ each team has no fewer than 10 and no more than 20 members.

Once these were applied, only 1,500 of the 3,000 Head Office employees were considered eligible. These staff were then subdivided into teams of 10–20 according to a specific distinction – for example, in pensions they were initially split into North and South, and then further subdivided by the allocation of postcode areas until manageable and eligibly-sized teams were determined.

Each team was then targeted on

☐ cost
☐ speed of turnaround of policies
☐ quality of service – as judged by formal surveys of customer satisfaction.

Within each team, individual performance is mostly judged against

☐ the number of policies processed
☐ the percentage accuracy
☐ a subjective measure relating to team effectiveness and harmony.

Pay rises for teams are set in a similar manner to individual increases, as described earlier. Once the overall kitty is established, each functional head has a defined amount of money to distribute. He or she then rates each of the departments according to the five criteria used in the appraisal system. A proportion of the kitty is allocated to each performance rating – eg rating 1 might receive ten shares, 2 perhaps eight, 3 perhaps six, etc. In some years, if overall performance is poor and the kitty therefore limited, it could be that departments rated as good (level 3) receive nothing because, although they performed well, other departments performed better in difficult times.

The departmental managers are thus allocated a fund, and they rate the overall team performance against the same criteria. The individual performance appraisal then comes into effect as a measure of contribution to the team and individual development.

It is generally felt that the performance management and performance-related pay systems for both individual and team-based work operate reasonably well. The downsides of team-based pay are, possibly,

- [ ] a downward spiral by which a lower-performing team receives less money and is therefore unable to attract the better staff
- [ ] good staff migrate to the best teams, where the best rewards are available
- [ ] the mathematics of the scheme can be quite complicated

Gareth Trevor has learned some specific lessons during the transition:

- [ ] you can't pay for performance if you can't measure it
- [ ] merit pay should not be used as an incentive but as a reward
- [ ] people have to be paid to come to work – but team spirit, comradeship and the sense of achievement are possibly greater motivators
- [ ] communicate, communicate and communicate again
- [ ] involve staff from the beginning and throughout the process: generally, people like to be involved in how their work is organised, and the team-based approach achieves exactly that.

9

BRINGING IT ALL TOGETHER: A CASE STUDY AND SOME CONCLUSIONS

Mike Walters

In writing about performance management, we have applied a number of principles drawn from our experience of working as managers and consultants with a wide range of organisations. These principles are implicit, in one way or another, in each of the preceding chapters, but in conclusion it may be helpful to tease out some of the key themes. To illustrate these themes we have also provided a case study designed to demonstrate the practical applications (as well as some of the potential pitfalls).

We have assumed that in virtually every contemporary organisation the application of performance management has a dual focus. First, there is a need to ensure that all employees maintain certain specified minimum standards of performance. In a world where competitive advantage is increasingly defined by the twin goals of quality and efficiency – in other words, meeting the customer's needs as precisely, quickly and cheaply as possible – few organisations are able to tolerate substandard performance. Increasingly, therefore, performance management techniques are being used to ensure that clear performance standards are defined and delivered.

But performance management is not simply about delivering minimum standards. In an increasingly volatile operating environment, most organisations cannot afford to stand still. For these organisations, performance management is also a tool to deliver continuous improvement. We are not simply looking for employees to maintain the same standards as last year or last week. We are looking for them continually to improve what they do and how they do it. If it is applied effectively, performance management can be used not only to define ever more challenging targets but also to provide employees with the support and capability needed to achieve them.

As we have repeatedly stressed in the course of this book, however, performance management cannot be carried out in a vacuum. Individual performance and performance improvement are meaningful only against a background of defined organisational direction, goals, targets and values. If we do not know where the organisation is going or what the organisation needs, there is little point in our trying to manage the performance of its individual members. Equally, how can we know what mechanisms are likely to support improved performance, if we do not know what kind of performance we are seeking?

This sounds obvious, and yet all too often approaches to performance management begin at the bottom – with the application of an 'off-the-shelf' tool – an appraisal scheme, a training programme, or some form of performance-related pay scheme. At best, the tool is applied in isolation, unsupported by activities or developments elsewhere in the organisation. At worst, the tools may be actively contradictory to the wider goals or needs of the organisation. It is all too common for us to see, for example, organisations struggling to develop more effective teamworking while simultaneously pushing through a bonus scheme based exclusively on individual performance.

We suggest instead, therefore, that performance has to begin at the top – with the clear definition of organisational objectives, targets, needs, priorities and culture. Only when these have been defined is it possible to develop the particular mixture of techniques, systems and measures that will support the performance improvements needed. In other words, there is no right way to manage and improve performance. A performance management strategy that is appropriate for, say, a commercial business looking to expand aggressively into new markets is likely to be entirely inappropriate for a public sector body looking to optimise the quality and efficiency of its services. Although the two organisations might well have some characteristics and needs in common, the thoughtless transposition of performance management techniques from one to the other may well lead only to inappropriate behaviours, demotivated employees and an ineffective organisation.

Our model of performance management is therefore essentially a contingent one. Developing the performance pyramid featured in Chapter 1, we might derive a schema of performance management as in Figure 11 – with examples of potential tools and techniques shown down the right-hand side.

Figure 11

IDEALISED PERFORMANCE MANAGEMENT

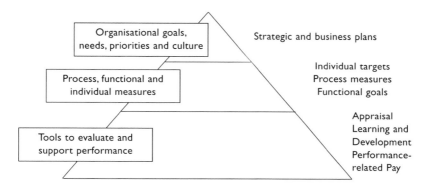

The practical implications of this model are best understood by examining how it can be applied in a case study organisation. The case study that follows is, as a totality, fictitious. In putting it together, we have nonetheless drawn heavily on our experiences as managers and consultants with a wide variety of public and private sector organisations. Most of the issues, approaches and problems discussed in the case study are therefore based on real experiences.

Case study: A2Z Travel

A2Z Travel is a newly formed company that provides bus and coach services in various parts of the UK. The company runs a number of scheduled services between major cities, but also provides leisure excursion services to tourist resorts on both a scheduled and a custom basis. The company is a wholly-owned subsidiary of a formerly public-sector transport company that has recently been privatised. Until recent years the parent organisation had not operated in a commercial environment and had not had to face external competition. It had struggled – not always successfully – to cope with the competitive pressures arising from public transport deregulation. Although the parent organisation's business performance improved over the previous year, its initial performance as a commercial business was relatively weak.

In part, the former uncompetitiveness of the parent company reflected the limitations of its corporate structures and practices. Its culture tended to be very conservative, its human resource practices and policies drawn largely from a local authority model, a generally high level of bureaucracy evident in most of its processes. The organisation had not traditionally made any link between the employees' pay and individual or corporate performance. The majority of employees had been on either fixed wages (the 'rate for the job') or on guaranteed incremental salary ranges. Among waged staff, overtime tended to be high, and many employees were able to obtain significant wage supplements through shift-working and through a complex system of allowance payments. Union membership in the organisation was high (over 80 per cent), and management recognised several unions representing different categories of staff.

Against this background, the new company was formed to provide services in the highly competitive leisure market, operating as a rival to a number of long-established competitors. From the inception of the new company, there was an awareness that if it were to compete effectively in this market it had to develop standards of performance – in terms, for example, of customer service, flexibility, responsiveness, cost efficiency and reliability – that were considerably higher than those so far achieved by its parent. This in turn required the development both of an appropriate culture and values, and of the practical tools needed to manage performance.

The new company employed some 400 staff across the country. Of these, around 200 were drivers, around 100 marketing, sales and customer service staff, and the remainder were administrative, management and support staff of various kinds. Although the company had been established as a new enterprise, in practice around half of its workforce (including a majority of the drivers) were recruited from the parent organisation. There was therefore a perceived danger of importing the culture of the parent organisation into the new company. Against this background, therefore, the new company's first priority was to establish a framework for managing the performance of its workforce that would support the company's challenging business goals.

Phase One: understanding the need

In the parent organisation, performance management had been an extremely limited process. Although the organisation had operated an appraisal scheme for management grades, it had been a largely impressionistic activity – managers simply asked to provide narrative descriptions of their subordinates' performance. The scheme had not fed into any form of systematic training needs analysis, and – except in cases of extreme poor performance – had had no effect on the allocation of annual incremental pay rises. For other categories of staff, performance management had been virtually non-existent.

From the formation of the new company, therefore, its senior management team identified the need for a much more systematic and comprehensive approach to performance management. Initial discussions in this area highlighted several broad needs:

- ☐ the need for formal performance appraisal for all staff
- ☐ the need for some formal link between pay and performance, whether at an individual or a corporate level
- ☐ the need to ensure that the workforce had the skills and commitment to deliver the objectives of the new company
- ☐ the need to ensure that the company was able to measure its progress in improving the workforce's performance and capability.

At this stage, the implications of these broad objectives were still far from clear. The senior team, for example, was uncertain about precisely what kinds of skills and capability would be required by the company, or about how the need for these skills would vary between different categories of staff. To what extent, for example, would drivers or administrative staff require customer service skills? To what extent would sales and marketing staff require an understanding of the operational aspects of the business? There was also a lack of clarity about the company's pay requirements. In the first place, the senior team was convinced that there ought to be a greater link between pay and performance. At a very basic level – because the company would be facing unprecedented competition – it would be unable to afford automatic pay increases if they were not matched by an equivalent improvement in corporate performance. Alongside this, though, there was also a perceived need to use the pay system to encourage qualities required by the new organisation – for example, multi-skilling, increased flexibility, and higher day-to-day levels of performance. Finally, at a practical level, the company also wished to move away from high levels of overtime and allowance payments. The latter area, in particular, had degenerated into a mass of 'Spanish customs' – many staff receiving allowances for reasons of history rather than of performance.

In the face of these various requirements the company was unsure whether it should adopt some form of performance pay linked to profit or to corporate performance, whether it should focus on individual contribution, or whether it should develop some combination of the two. At the individual level, the company questioned whether the pay system should reward quantifiable measures of output (such as sales, completion of journeys to schedule, and so on), or whether it should address inputs (for example, the acquisition of multiple skills or new competencies). All of these issues were potentially attractive in helping to meet the company's needs – but it was not clear how they should be prioritised.

The company was equally unsure about how performance appraisal should be applied. There was considerable dissatisfaction with the parent company's scheme, which was perceived to be hugely unhelpful in improving individual performance. There was some feeling that the appraisal scheme should be linked directly to performance pay in order to help promote a new 'culture of performance'. Others argued, however, that the purpose of appraisal should be to help individuals to improve their own performance, and that this would inevitably be constrained if individuals were aware that the appraisal was linked directly to pay.

With all of these various issues in mind, therefore, the company's first task was to devote serious attention to the identification of its key business priorities. After reviewing the parent company arrangements, the subsidiary company felt that it had an opportunity to adopt a radical approach that would suit its particular needs. For example, union resistance was much less of an issue in the new company. The company continued to recognise the same unions as its parent organisation (although it adopted a more streamlined 'single table' approach to bargaining) but made clear that recognition would be dependent on the unions' providing flexible responses to the company's commercial requirements. From discussion with the unions it was evident that there would be little serious objection to the establishment of new working practices in what was effectively a 'greenfield' operation.

The senior team therefore quickly acknowledged that there was a need to develop a customised approach to performance management that fully reflected the company's distinct needs. Although the company had already developed a substantial business plan, the senior team soon discovered that this was only the first stage towards understanding the company's priorities and needs. Up till then, for example, the business planning process had given little consideration to the human resource implications of its various strategies and objectives. It was not clear precisely what kinds of performance or behaviour would be needed to deliver the business goals and targets that were set out in the plan.

Using the business plan as a basis, therefore, the senior team arranged an 'away-day', facilitated by external consultants, in which they explored in depth the performance implications of their business goals. At the end of this process they succeeded in identifying a number of broad performance priorities which applied – to varying degrees – across all parts of the organisation. These were:

- [ ] improved reliability in delivering the core customer service (for example, reduced cancellations or late running)
- [ ] improved productivity and cost efficiency in carrying out all organisational activities
- [ ] improved customer service both in providing the core transport services and in support areas such as the provision of timetable or schedule information or the handling of queries and complaints.

Alongside these broad objectives the company also identified several specific requirements which applied to particular groups of staff (but which also carried potential implications for the wider workforce). For example, there was a need to identify new products and services, as well as ways of enhancing existing services, in order to maintain an edge in a highly competitive market. In addition, there was a need to improve the marketing and selling of the company's services. Traditionally, the parent company's approach to marketing and sales had been relatively low-key and reactive. For the new company, a much more aggressive approach was required.

Phase Two: developing the performance measures
Having identified its key business priorities, the senior team then proceeded to develop its detailed understanding of each of these priority areas. With the help of external consultants, a series of extended interviews was carried out with managers and employees in all parts of the business, exploring the precise meaning and implications of the business's key goals across the organisation. What, for example, did 'reliability' mean to a driver? What was his or her understanding of the standards of reliability required by the company, and how well did these match the expectations of senior management? What were the major barriers to reliability, and which of these lay outside the driver's control?

Similar questions were asked about the two other core areas – cost efficiency and customer services – and from the responses the company rapidly built up a three-dimensional picture of performance issues and concerns across the organisation. Overall, the company gathered information in a number of areas:

- how well the company's key business needs and priorities were understood in different parts and at different levels in the organisation
- how performance in these priority areas was currently measured and managed (for example, how in practice local managers or supervisors evaluated the performance of their staff)
- the major perceived barriers to improving performance in the priority areas.

The company quickly uncovered a number of critical performance issues. First, it was evident that the company's performance priorities were not clearly or consistently understood across the organisation. In many cases, for example, local managers and staff were applying unacceptably low standards of performance in areas such as reliability and customer service. Indeed, few local managers had established any reliable measures of performance in these areas. In the parent company, little data had been gathered about operational performance, and most managers had little idea how to assess their own local performance or to evaluate how this compared with other parts of the business.

It was also evident that the barriers to performance improvement were both numerous and highly varied. Although most employees seemed committed to the success of the new company, there was considerable evidence that many staff at all levels lacked the skills and competencies required to deliver improved performance. In particular, there was evidence of a shortage of managerial and supervisory skill among managers who, in the parent company, had tended to be promoted on the basis either of technical skills or simply on a 'buggins's turn' basis. There was also evidence that many front-line staff, including both drivers and front-desk sales staff, lacked customer service skills. In the parent company these employees had not traditionally seen their role as providing a service to a customer who might take his or her business elsewhere.

There was also some evidence that performance problems were occurring as a result of poor service from outside the company. For example, the company's maintenance work was handled on a contract basis by the parent organisation. The resulting service was often slow, unreliable, and of poor quality, resulting for instance, in buses being unavailable or breaking down. Although the blame for these problems might lie outside the company, the senior team was aware that this could not excuse poor performance to its own customers. It was therefore necessary to look at ways of improving the quality of external service received. In the first instance the senior team believed that this could best be achieved by improving its own skills in managing external contractors.

Having gathered and analysed this data, the senior team began to develop some key measures of organisational performance designed to reflect its own defined priorities. The aim was to identify the key indicators that were expected to underpin continuous improvement in business performance. Key measures included

☐ a formal measure of service reliability, defined in terms of both service provision and punctuality (ie whether the bus ran and whether it was on time): measurement focused on identifying the proportion of services that did not meet acceptable reliability standards

☐ formal measures of productivity and cost efficiency, based on reviewing the levels of staffing and other resources needed to deliver defined units of service.

☐ formal measures of customer satisfaction: the company recognised that customer satisfaction is not simply about achieving quantitative performance standards but may also reflect more emotional and less rational aspects of interaction with the customer; for instance, even though the bus arrives on time, the customer may be dissatisfied if he or she feels that the driver has been rude or abrupt – the company therefore introduced qualitative measures of customer satisfaction, based on customer surveys conducted among both actual and potential customers.

The company applied these measures hierarchically so that they could be broken down to provide a 'snapshot' of performance at each level in the organisation. A consistent 'basket' of measures was applied at the corporate level, within each geographical division, and in local offices. This enabled the company to compare levels of performance between different parts of the organisation.

There was an acknowledgement that levels of performance might legitimately vary between different offices because of, for example, different geographical or market characteristics. The aim therefore was that comparison should not be used to penalise offices but rather to provide management with the basis for exploring the reasons for variation in performance. In practice, however, this proved to be one of the most difficult aspects of the whole process. Many local managers, because they had been accustomed to working in an environment of high control and low trust, perceived the measures as 'league tables' and so tended to react defensively. In responding to this, there was an onus on senior management to respond sensitively and constructively, rather than penalising below-average performance. Both parties experienced difficulty in responding to these challenges, although the application of the measures improved significantly over time.

Alongside these general corporate performance measures, the company also identified a number of specific measures for more specialist groups. These included, for example, targets for new product/service development, sales targets, and measures of public awareness of the company and its services.

Phase Three: developing the appraisal and pay schemes

Having identified the core performance measures for the organisation, the company then began to develop its processes for individual performance appraisal. Given the nature of its performance needs – and in particular the perceived need not merely to achieve quantitative improvements in operational and business performance but also to make qualitative changes in the competencies and values of the workforce – the company decided to adopt an approach with a dual focus. The appraisal scheme was designed to assess the individual's performance both against defined performance or development targets (the 'what') and against defined stylistic or cultural requirements (the 'how'). In other words, the individual would be evaluated at the highest level only if he or she was doing *the right things in the right way*.

To support this process, the company began by developing a

framework of the behavioural competencies required from employees. The aim was to provide a definition of the types of behaviour that would be displayed by an effective performer in the company – for example, in areas such as teamworking, customer service, flexibility, and so on. The definitions were developed through a series of interviews and focus groups with individuals and managers at all levels in the organisation. The key questions, in simple terms, were 'What kind of performance do we want from individuals in this company?', and 'What does this performance *look like* when we see it?' The intention was to move away from broad generalisations and abstractions towards a precise and practical definition of the behaviour that was required.

The resulting appraisal was a two-dimensional matrix. The manager had first to review the individual against the behavioural competencies required for the individual's role in the company. The manager would then review the individual's performance against performance or 'contribution' targets which had been agreed at the previous appraisal. Managers were encouraged to set contribution objectives that supported the three key organisational priorities (although other objectives could also be set to meet specific local needs). Managers were also encouraged to set 'stretch' targets that would challenge the individual.

The individual was then rated against the two dimensions of this matrix. The rating matrix was constructed so that slightly greater weighting was given to the demonstration of the required behavioural competencies (on the basis that an individual behaving in the appropriate way should in the longer term produce the required contribution). To encourage continuous development and the setting of 'stretch' objectives, the rating also placed a relatively high weighting on making significant progression towards a contribution target that was not necessarily achieved. The aim was to move away from a mechanistic obsession with quantitative targets (in relation to which, for example, an individual who has made significant progress might be judged to have 'failed' because he or she has narrowly missed a pre-defined target) towards a more positive focus on development.

Finally, the appraisal process required the manager and

appraisee to agree the competence and contribution goals for the coming year, and to identify the development required to support these.

Following the initial development and piloting of the appraisal process, there was an extended debate within the company about the extent to which the process should be linked to pay. Some felt strongly that – for the reasons discussed earlier – the company needed quickly to establish a performance-related pay scheme. Others were concerned that the introduction of such a scheme would undermine the development potential of the appraisal process. Eventually it was decided that a performance pay scheme was needed – not least, to provide an explicit demonstration that the company was operating in a new commercial environment and so must apply tight commercial disciplines – but that some care was needed in linking this to the appraisal process.

After some initial consideration of the various performance pay options open to the company – including for example developmental options such as gainsharing or value-added schemes – the company decided to adopt a relatively simple approach. In particular, the company wished to apply a scheme that would be readily and easily understood by all employees. At the corporate level, the general level of annual increase – that is, the available budget – was to be explicitly linked to company performance, although not through a fixed formula. At the individual level, within the available budget, the level of performance was to be explicitly linked to the rating produced by the matrix. It was felt that this kind of explicit link would provide greater transparency (and reinforce the critical link between individual and corporate performance) than if the pay and appraisal processes were kept artificially separate. At the same time, as indicated above, the rating scheme was weighted so that the major emphasis was placed on the demonstration of the required competencies and on evidence of significant progress, rather than on the achievement or non-achievement of one-dimensional targets. In this way, it was hoped that the use of performance pay would not become a barrier to personal and performance development.

Phase Four: responding to the performance management process

Once the appraisal scheme was in place, the company recognised that it would need to find effective ways of responding to the development needs of individuals. Responses were developed in several ways. First, the organisational competency framework provided a consistent tool for assessing the overall development needs of the organisation. The HR department was able to aggregate the competence development needs of the company's employees, and so identify a number of priority areas for development activity. This included, for example, specific training in customer service and in supervisory skills.

At the individual level, managers were encouraged to identify a range of development opportunities in addition to formal training. In particular, where appropriate, managers were encouraged to agree a formal personal development plan with the individual that would reflect the individual's needs and preferred learning style. This could mix formal training, on-the-job learning, temporary secondments, and so on. The company is still debating whether to extend the personal developing planning process to all staff. The current feeling is that the process is resource-intensive – managers requiring a high level of support from HR – and that it is likely to be most effective if it is targeted on those that are most likely to benefit. At the same time there is a recognition that at present some staff may be failing to fulfil their potential because of the absence of a comprehensive scheme.

Finally, the company is continuing to review the effectiveness of its overall performance management process. In general, views of the process are very positive, and there is a belief that it has played a major part in enabling the organisation to meet the challenges of its competitive environment. At the same time there is an awareness that the process can be further refined and developed. The competence framework in particular needs to be further revised as the company's needs have developed. The company is also considering the potential benefits of upwards appraisal as a tool to help improve management and supervisory performance, although there is a recognition that some will feel uncomfortable with this.

There is also a specific debate about whether more focused

performance standards, measures and payment systems need to be developed in areas such as sales, marketing and new product development. At present, although specific measures have been developed in these areas, their performance has been managed simply through the general scheme. There is, for example, no additional sales incentive or commission scheme for sales staff. The initial feeling was that, given the culture shock already being experienced by the organisation, further developments would probably be counter-productive. Nevertheless, now that employees are becoming accustomed to the broad concepts of performance management, consideration is being given to the possible benefits of introducing more specific schemes for particular groups. At the same time, some have expressed concern that such schemes might prove divisive and might undermine some of the benefits that have already been achieved.

The company recognises that there is no simply answer to these questions, and that it can only continue to review its measures of performance against the organisation's needs. At the corporate level, similarly, its business goals and priorities will continue to change as the company and its operating environment develops. Most importantly of all, the company has formally acknowledged, as a key priority for its senior management team, both the importance of performance management and the need for continuous review and development of the performance management process

Our case study demonstrates the extent to which performance management must be customised to meet the needs of the specific organisation. In responding to the contingencies of individual organisations, however, it is not true that anything goes. In the preceding chapters, and in our case study, we have articulated a number of issues, principles and guidelines, that are perhaps worth summarising:

□ First, once we have defined the organisational context within which the performance management strategy is being developed, we need systematically to identify an appropriate basket of measures at different levels and in different parts of the organisation. As Peter Lawson's model indicates, we need measures that are both internally and externally focused. We need to look both at our internal efficiency and effectiveness, and at our how we are perceived externally by our customers, partners, suppliers, stakeholders and competitors. We also need measures that are hierarchical, so that we can understand clearly how the performance of individual functions, processes and employees contribute to the overall performance of the organisation.

☐ Alongside this, we need to ensure that the mix and balance of the measures we apply appropriately matches our corporate needs and objectives. Performance is rarely monolithic, and for most of us it involves juggling a variety of disparate and sometimes contradictory goals. We need to work quickly but still produce high-quality outputs. We need to hit our sales targets but ensure that our profit margins are not unduly squeezed. We need to work collaboratively but still take responsibility for our own performance. Often this involves balance and compromise, and this needs to be reflected in the measures and targets we apply. If we get the balance wrong, or if we unduly emphasise one measures at the expense of others, we are likely to encourage inappropriate behaviour. Moreover, while it is true that performance measurement is likely to be an evolving process – which we will continue to review and improve – it is also true that bad performance measurement is worse than none at all. If we measure the wrong things, we encourage people to do the wrong things, and ultimately this results in a dysfunctional organisation.

☐ Increasingly we need to look not just at functional performance but also at process performance. In other words, we need to look at the overall sequence of activities, perhaps covering several functions or divisions that deliver the required output – a product or service – to our customers. This in turn means that we need to deliver measures of customer satisfaction, and that we need to be able to track these back along the process so that we can evaluate performance at each key stage. We need to identify those points in the process where value is being added, and we need to understand how these relate to the ultimate delivery to the customer. We also need to understand how these measures of customer service and satisfaction relate to our corporate needs and objectives.

☐ This increasing focus on process delivery also carries a number of implications for the establishment of individual performance measures. In many cases, for example, individuals may be accountable for the performance of processes or other activities over which they do not have full control. In order to meet process goals, for example, a manager may have to liaise with managers and employees in a range of functions, with no direct supervisory authority. Again, therefore, we need to understand the nature of these interdependencies, and be aware that overall performance may need to be managed as much through collaboration and co-operation as through direction and control. This carries implications both for the kinds of measures and targets we set, and for how we support individuals to deliver these.

☐ As organisational needs and structures grow increasingly complex, so the definition of individual performance goals and measures also grows ever more problematic. We need to identify measures that not only reflect organisational needs and priorities, but that also take account of the nature of the individual's contribution. Do we require the individual to be innovative, or are we simply looking for incremental improvements in current service? Are we looking for the individual to be a change agent, or are we seeking someone who will consolidate existing performance? Do we wish to reward past achievement or is it appropriate to recognise potential? How quickly are we expecting the individual to produce results, and over what time-scale should we measure his or her performance? There are no simple answers to any of these questions, but we need to look carefully both at what the organisation requires from the individual and at how we expect the individual to react to the measures we have set. We need to ensure that the individual understands and accepts the nature of the contribution we are expecting. And, above all, we need to ensure that we apply the measures, not as a punitive process, but as a tool to support continuing performance improvement.

☐ In practice, appraisal is likely to be the core mechanism we use to help translate performance measures into improved individual performance. There are countless ways of approaching appraisal – and the preferred approach reflects not only the organisation's needs but also its culture and history – but we suggest that the ideal is 360-degree appraisal. In other words, appraisal should be carried out not simply by the individual's boss, but also by his or her peers, subordinates, and other relevant colleagues. The process should be forward-looking, its focus on performance improvement, and should be underpinned by clear and precise information about corporate and individual needs and goals. In line with our broader model of performance management it should incorporate measures of both output and behaviour (the 'what' and the 'how').

☐ If it is to provide the basis for genuine performance improvement, the appraisal process needs to be linked to a systematic process of personal development planning. This should focus on the question 'What should I be able to do?', and should reflect a collaboration between the individual and the organisation, although the individual should increasingly take responsibility for his or her develop-ment. We recommend a four-stage approach that looks at

  – the individual's current skills, competencies, interests and values in relation to his or her current role and expected future development needs

  – the external factors influencing the organisation, and their likely impact on individual development needs

  – the establishment of a development plan, based on an analysis of these needs and opportunities, including standards and measures of development and the types and level of support that are needed

  – the monitoring of the delivery of the action plan, and the identification and resolution of any barriers to delivery.

The delivery of the personal development plan, in most cases, requires effective individual learning and development. The relationship between learning and performance improvement, however, is often far from straightforward. Even if we can be sure that learning has occurred, there may be many barriers to its practical application in the workplace. Effective learning is likely to be a cyclical process, involving both experiential and conceptual stages. If we are to be successful both in ensuring that learning takes place and that it is translated into practical performance improvement, we need to develop organisations that encourage and assist individuals to progress through this cycle and that provide individuals with the opportunities to apply their learning in practice.

Finally, we addressed the controversial role of pay in supporting (or undermining) performance improvement. Although there is little doubt that pay can be applied as a tool to influence behaviours and culture, it is also true that the relationship between pay and performance is more complex and problematic than is often assumed. Above all, there is a need to ensure that the reward strategy is aligned with the wider performance management strategy – and that, in turn, means that it must be aligned with the needs, goals and priorities of the organisation. Like the appraisal process, it must reflect both the 'what' and the 'how' – behaviours and styles, and the delivery of outputs and objectives.

Performance management is never a simple process. There are no cast-iron rules, and there are no patent solutions to apply. As the pace of organisational change increases, the challenges become greater still. We need to develop measures and approaches that support not just the delivery of today's objectives but also the development we need to meet the needs of tomorrow. We need to ensure high performance, but we also need to encourage flexibility and innovation. We need to establish robust and reliable performance management processes, but we also need continually to be reviewing and developing these as organisational circumstances change. This is undoubtedly a major challenge, but we hope that this book has provided at least some of the understanding needed to meet it.

FURTHER READING

ARGYRIS C. AND SCHON D. *Organisational Learning – A Theory of Action Perspective*, London, Addison–Wesley (1978).

BARON A AND WALTERS M. *The Culture Factor*. London, Institute of Personnel and Development (1994).

BASS B.M. AND VAUGHAN J.A. *Training in Industry: The Management of Learning*. London, Tavistock Publications (Behavioural Science in Industry Series) (1967).

BURGOYNE J. *'Doubts about Competencies'*. M. Devine (ed.) *The Photofit Manager*, London, Unwin Hyman, (1990).

CANNELL M. AND WOOD S. *Incentive Pay – Impact and Evolution*. London, Institute of Personnel and Development (1992).

DALZIEL AND ANDERSON *Learning Styles of Students from Different Disciplines* (as yet unpublished research). Glasgow, Glasgow Caledonian University (1994).

DIXON N. *The Organisational Learning Cycle – How we can Learn Collectively*. Maidenhead, McGraw-Hill (1994).

DRENNAN D. *Transforming Company Culture*. Maidenhead, McGraw-Hill (1992).

FISHER M. *Performance Appraisals*. The *Sunday Times* Business Skills Series. London, Kogan Page (1995).

FLETCHER C. AND WILLIAMS R. *Performance Appraisal and Career Development*. London, Hutchinson (1985).

FLETCHER C. *Appraisal – Routes to Improved Performance*. London, Institute of Personnel Management (1993).

GARRATT B. *Creating a Learning Organisation*. Hemel Hempstead, Director Books (1990).

GARRATT B. *The Learning Organisation*. Aldershot, Gower (1987).

GOOLD M. AND QUINN J. *Strategic Control: Milestones for Long-term Performance*. London, Economist Books (1990).

GUNN T.G. *Manufacturing for Competitive Advantage –*

Becoming a World Class Manufacturer. Ballinger (1987).

HARPER S. *Measuring Business Performance*. Aldershot, Gower (1994).

HEDBERG B.O. *How Organisations Learn and Unlearn*, Handbook of Organisation Design, Vol. 1, Paul C. Nystrom and William H. Starbuck (eds.). Oxford, Oxford University Press (1981).

HERMANN N. *The Creative Brain*. Brain Books, 2nd edition (1992).

HONEY P. AND MUMFORD A. *Manual of Learning Styles*. Honey (1982).

HONEY P. AND MUMFORD A. *Manual of Learning Opportunities*. Honey (1989).

HONEY P. *Solving People Problems*. Maidehead, McGraw-Hill (1980).

HUMAN *Educating and Developing Managers for a Changing South Africa*. Juta & Co. Limited (1991).

HUNTER *Three by Three Model for Cultural Change* (unpublished MBA Dissertation). Glasgow Caledonian University.

JONES A. AND HENDRY C. *The Learning Organisation*. Human Resource Development Partnership (1992).

KESSLER I. AND PURCELL J. *The Templeton Performance-Related Pay Project: Summary of Key Findings*, Management Research Paper 94/3. Templeton College (1993).

KOLB D.A., RUBIN I.M. AND MCINTYRE J.M. *Organisational Psychology: An Experiential Approach*. Hemel Hempstead, Prentice Hall (1974).

LONG P. *Performance Appraisal Revisited*. London, Institute of Personnel Management (1986).

MADDUX R.B. *Effective Performance Appraisals*. London, Kogan Page (1987).

MARTIN D. Whole Brain Teaching and Learning, *Training and Development* (August 1994).

MAYER H.H., KAYE, E. AND FRENCH J.P.R. Split Roles in Performance Appraisal. *Harvard Business Review* (1985).

PEDLER M. AND BOYDELL T. *Managing Yourself*. London, Fontana (1987).

PEDLER M., BOYDELL T. AND BURGOYNE J. *Towards the Learning Company Management Education & Development* Volume 20 (1989).

PHILIP T. *Making Performance Appraisal Work.* Maidenhead, McGraw-Hill (1983).

RANDELL G. et al. *Staff Appraisal: A First Step to Effective Leadership.* London, Institute of Personnel Management, 3rd Edition (1984).

REISANS R. *The Origin and Growth of Action Learning.* Bromley, Chartwell-Bratt (1985).

RUMMLER G.A. AND BRACHE A.P. *Improving Performance: How to Manage the White Space on the Organisation Chart.* Jossey (1990).

SENGE P.M. *The Fifth Discipline: The Art and Practice of the Learning Organisation.* London, Century Business (1992).

STEWART V. AND STEWART A. *Managing the Poor Performer.* Aldershot, Gower Update (1988).

SWIERINGA J. AND WIERDSMA A. *Becoming a Learning Organisation – Beyond the Learning Curve.* London, Addison–Wesley (1992).

WALTERS M. *What About the Workers? – Making Employee Surveys Work.* London, Institute of Personnel Management (1990).

WALTERS M. *Building the Responsive Organisation.* Maidenhead, McGraw-Hill (1993).

WILLIAMS A., DOBSON P. AND WALTERS M. *Changing Culture,* London, Institute of Personnel Management, 2nd edition (1993).

WILSON T.B. *Innovative Reward Systems for the Changing Workplace.* Maidenhead, McGraw-Hill (1995).

INDEX